GIS Mapping for Public Safety

First Edition

By
Joel M. Caplan
William D. Moreto

RUTGERS
Center on Public Security

Newark
New Jersey
USA

This entire book is available to anyone for free download at www.rutgerscps.org

Suggested Citation:
Caplan, J. M. & Moreto, W. D. (2012). *GIS Mapping for Public Safety, First Edition*. Newark, NJ: Rutgers Center on Public Security.

Produced by Rutgers Center on Public Security:
Based at the Rutgers University School of Criminal Justice, the Rutgers Center on Public Security (RCPS) offers a multidisciplinary approach to the academic study and practical application of ways in which democratic societies can effectively address crime, terrorism and other threats to public security. This involves the prevention of, protection from and response to natural or human-made events that could endanger the safety or security of people or property in a given area. RCPS engages in innovative data analysis and information dissemination, including the use of GIS, for strategic decision-making and tactical action. Visit RCPS online for current research projects, reports and publications.

www.rutgerscps.org

Acknowledgements

The opinions expressed in this book are the views of the authors and do not necessarily reflect the views and opinions of the Rutgers Center on Public Security, Rutgers University, or the School of Criminal Justice.

Table of Contents

PREFACE

WHAT IS PUBLIC SAFETY?

Public safety means programs carried out or promoted for public purposes and benefit. This involves, directly or indirectly, the prevention of, protection from, and/or response to natural or human-made events that could endanger the safety or security of people or property in a given area[1]. Public safety embraces an interdisciplinary framework to address these threats and respond to the needs of the general public.

USING GIS FOR PUBLIC SAFETY

Considering the spatial context of activities and events is important because everyone operates in space. This is a simple idea, but it is often overlooked. Think about it: your activities, legal and illegal, happen at some location on Earth. Therefore, public safety and individual risk can change with the geography—whether it is one side of a street or one side of town.

A Geographic Information System (GIS) is a tool that adds the dimension of spatial analysis to research and evaluation by providing an interface between data and a map. GIS has proven to be an ideal platform for the convergence of public safety-specific information in relation to historical events, natural or human-made disasters, vulnerable populations, and critical infrastructure key to a community's sustainability. Data and information in different formats from different locations can be integrated and displayed in GIS. The data can be quickly queried, analyzed, and communicated through a map. It can then be easily disseminated, understood and acted on.

ABOUT THIS BOOK

This book focuses on Esri's ArcGIS functionality and presents tools and procedures that are commonly used by public safety researchers and practitioners. It gives simple steps for descriptive, exploratory, and explanatory mapping tasks and includes concise but meaningful discussions to let you critically assess and accurately apply the software to your own unique specialty. This provides a solid foundation for advanced spatial thinking and permits you to utilize GIS technology in your own innovative ways. This book is intended for an introductory audience, but GIS users at all skill levels can find value in it as a reference manual. "Introductory" does not mean limited content. Rather, it means that the focus of the book is on the technical aspects of GIS mapping rather than the conceptual or theoretical.

If you do not already own ArcGIS software, you may download a free 60-day trial copy at www.esri.com. The download includes a full version of the software and all extensions discussed herein. If you are a student with a valid ID card, you might also consider purchasing the software at the discounted educational rate.

Note that the map display (Data View), toolbars and other screen captures throughout this book may differ slightly from your own computer screen. Attempts were made to use default settings; however, in some circumstances, examples are displayed in more meaningful ways for demonstration purposes.

HOW TO USE THIS BOOK

Generally speaking, arrows ("➔") indicate moving to the next step in a sequence of steps. For example, see below how to open ArcMap 10 from the Windows Taskbar.

From Windows Taskbar: Start Menu ➔ ArcGIS ➔ ArcMap 10

The stepwise icon will be used to indicate technical steps. Key words/phrases within the steps will be bolded. For example:

 From the "**Symbology**" Tab, click the "**Categories**" option within the "**Show:**" box and select "**Unique values**".

A "Need-to-know" icon will be used to indicate important information about an ArcGIS tool, function, or procedure. Text associated with this icon will be italicized. For example:

 The Measure tool will use the display units you specified in the Data Frame Properties.

Case studies and practical examples that utilized a particular tool or procedure will be presented in ZOOM IN boxes, which appear as gray text boxes. For example:

ZOOM IN: Mapping Maritime Piracy Incidents With XY Coordinates

Web links will be functional if viewing this book in electronic (e.g., PDF) form. Links will appear as blue colored text. For example: The Risk Terrain Modeling Manual can be downloaded at www.riskterrainmodeling.com

PC OR MAC?

PC is preferred. ArcGIS by Esri is designed to run on a Microsoft Windows operating system. But with tools such as Parallels (www.parallels.com) or Boot Camp (part of MAC OS; www.apple.com), Intel-based Macintosh computer users can run ArcGIS products. Just use an external mouse or learn how to right-click. Right-clicking is required to access important menus in ArcGIS.

CHAPTER ONE

Introduction to Mapping and ArcGIS

WHAT IS GIS?

A geographic information system (GIS) is a computer software application for managing, editing, analyzing and displaying data which are spatially referenced to the Earth. Spatial data can be represented as individual layers, displayed as separate entities, or be combined with other layers to be displayed together[2].

Imagine a GIS as a high-tech overhead projector from the "old days" that used transparent plastic sheets and dry-erase markers as inputs that were then projected on a wall. If you think of each transparent sheet as a separate map layer, and you place all of the transparent sheets (map layers) on top of each other, you can see through all of them at-once. In this way, you can see relationships among the data that overlap in certain areas. Essentially, GIS does this digitally and in much more sophisticated ways.

Visualizing multiple map layers at once offers a means of exploring relationships among different data variables. For example, a map that only shows burglary points and absolutely no other data may not be particularly helpful. But, the burglary data can be layered with base maps that display the street network to show where these burglaries were committed. A third map layer could display all the properties across the area (e.g. owner occupied, rented, vacant buildings)[3]. These three layers might suggest that burglary incidents are highest on side streets—not major roadways—and in the areas where there is also a high percentage of vacant properties.

GIS COMPONENTS

A GIS has four components: hardware, software, people and data.

The bare minimum for **hardware** is a desktop or laptop computer. GIS hardware requirements might also include peripherals such as a printer, plotter, or scanner. Mobile phones, PDAs, computer tablets or GPS technology may also be used to synchronize data captured in the field to a central database[4].

Off-the-shelf GIS **software** products possess a wide range of functionality; though, software extensions can be added for advanced analysis and map production[5]. Some relevant software extensions for ArcGIS include Spatial Analyst or Crime Analysis Spatial Extension (CASE; http://www.crimeanalysts.net/case.htm). Specialist crime mapping software is also available such as GeoDa (http://geodacenter.asu.edu/), School COP (http://www.schoolcopsoftware.com), and CrimeStat (http://www.icpsr.umich.edu/CRIMESTAT). Quantum GIS (QGIS; http://www.qgis.org) is an Open Source GIS that runs on Linux, Unix, Mac OSX, and Windows. It supports numerous vector, raster, and database formats and functionalities, and it is free to download and use.

Operating a GIS involves bringing together the computer files that contain the data to be used, and possibly editing them, querying against them, linking them, adding new data and generating a display for output. A GIS requires trained **people** to perform these technical skills, as well as to ask spatial questions and interpret and communicate findings in meaningful and actionable ways[6].

Data must have a geographic reference such as street addresses or XY coordinates that can be used to link it to a map. Data collected via Excel, Access, Quattro Pro, Paradox, Oracle, SQL Server, or any other type of spreadsheet or database management system has potential for use in a GIS[7].

REPRESENTING OBJECTS (FEATURES) IN A GIS[8]

Spatial objects, or features, can be represented in three ways on a map: points, lines or polygons. **Points** can either be represented as a dot or other symbol. Locations of hospitals, for example, may be represented with the **H** symbol rather than a dot. **Lines (also known as polylines***)* are straight-line objects connecting two points. A polyline depicting a curved line (arc) is actually a series of straight segments. Lines can be displayed in a range of fonts (e.g. continuous or dashed lines) and in different colors and thicknesses[9]. Bus routes, streets, and rivers are usually represented using lines. A **polygon** is a closed area represented around its perimeter with a polyline. It exists as a solid object for the region it covers[10]. Police beats, counties, states, and ZIP Codes are examples of polygons.

ATTRIBUTE TABLES

Descriptive information about GIS features is stored in attribute tables. For example, an attribute table for point features representing crime incidents could include the crime type, the date of the crime, the time of the crime and the address of where the crime occurred. There is always one record in the attribute table that corresponds to each feature on the map. Attribute information can be used to view, select, analyze, and display features in a variety of ways on a map.

The attribute table and map features are linked together so that when a feature (e.g., point, line or polygon) is selected on the map, the attribute data for the feature is also selected (as shown below).

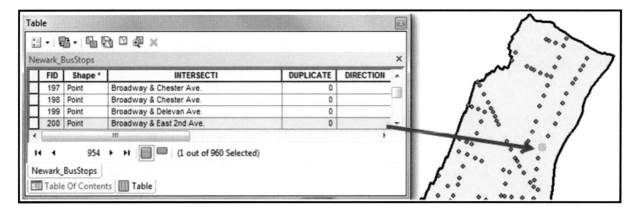

Attribute tables in a GIS will always have FID (Feature Identification) and Shape fields. This information is used to define the feature and the corresponding record in the attribute table so that a one-to-one correspondence is maintained between the feature on the map and its attribute record. Basically, attribute tables act as a key table between map features and additional information about each feature. Attribute tables support many fundamental GIS operations[11]: They organize and manage descriptive data about features. They are used for statistical summaries of descriptive data. Arithmetic and logic operations on rows and columns in tables are used to select features and to calculate new information for features. Tables are used to relate other information with map features.

DBF FILES

Attribute tables are stored in the dBase file format (.dbf). dBase was the first widely used database management system (DBMS) for microcomputers. The dBase DBMS was unique in that it provided a header section for describing the structure of the data in the file. This meant that the software program no longer required advance knowledge of the data structure, but rather, could ask the data file how it was structured. dBase gradually lost market share to competitors because it was slow to transition successfully to Microsoft Windows. Nevertheless, its underlying file format, the .dbf file, remains widely used in many contemporary applications that need a simple format to store structured data. The "shapefile" format for ArcGIS uses .dbf files to store feature attribute data.

TYPES OF GIS DATA

Tabular data: where you store attribute information about map features. ArcMap can only work with Excel (.xls), comma-delimited (.csv) and dBase (.dbf) files, so you will need to convert your tables to one of these formats before importing it to ArcMap.

Geographic data: Shapefiles are the standard format for geographic vector data in ArcGIS (see below). Raster GIS data is stored in GRID format, which is more similar to images.

Images: ArcGIS allows you to import and export many different types of images. The images you import may be scanned paper maps, aerial photos, or other pictures that you "hot link" to your map features. You can export finished maps from ArcGIS in a variety of formats: EMP, BMP, EPS, TIFF, PDF, JPEG, CGM, JPEG, PCX, and PNG.

VECTOR DATA AND SHAPEFILES

Vector is the most common GIS data type used in the social sciences. It uses points, lines, and polygons to represent map features. Vector data is excellent for representing discrete objects such as parcels, streets, and administrative boundaries. The vector format is not as good for representing things that vary continuously over space, such as temperature or elevation.

The **Shapefile** format was created by Esri (the maker of ArcGIS) in order to represent vector GIS data. Other GIS programs will use shapefiles, but geographic files from other GIS programs must be converted to shapefiles before ArcGIS applications can read them. As with other formats of geographic data, shapefiles link information about the location and shape of the map features to their attributes.

Shapefiles are made up of three or more files that need to be stored in the same directory in order for ArcGIS to recognize them. The most common files that comprise shapefiles are:

.shp - the file that stores the feature geometry (point ▓ , line ┳ , polygon ◲)

.shx - the file that stores the index of the feature geometry

.dbf - the dBASE file 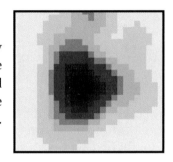 stores the attribute information of features. When a shapefile is added as a theme to a map view, this file is displayed as a feature table.

.sbn and .sbx - the files that store the spatial index of the features. These two files may not exist until you perform theme-on-theme selection, spatial join, or create an index on a theme's shape field.

.pjr – the file that stores information about the projection. This will only exist for shapefiles with defined projections.

The shapefile stores information about the shape of the map features, describing them in the "shape" field of the attribute table as point, line, or polygon. It also stores information about the real world location of each vertex that makes up the map features. Using this information, ArcGIS can perform spatial analyses.

RASTER DATA

Raster data use grids made up of equally-sized cells to represent spatially continuous data. Each cell is assigned real world coordinates and one attribute value (such as temperature or elevation). The user defines the cell size, allowing for very fine or course raster surfaces. Even when the cell size is very small, you can see the individual square cells when you zoom in. Raster grids cells are like pixels on a TV or computer screen.

Whereas shapefile-based map layers are oriented toward the depiction and analysis of discrete objects in space (represented as points, lines, or polygons), raster grids are oriented more toward the qualities of space itself. In order to work with raster data in ArcGIS, you need the Spatial Analyst extension. When raster layers have the same size cells, their values can be added, subtracted, multiplied, divided and queried using map algebra.

You can add raster data to ArcMap just as you do vector data, using the "Add Data" button. If the raster data have no spatial information (e.g. a scanned map), ArcMap will not be able to display it with other map layers. In this case, you may need to "georeference" the raster data.

ArcMap saves raster layers in its GRID format. ArcCatalog recognizes GRIDs and other image formats (including BMP, JPEG, TIFF) as raster layers. If you view a GRID outside of ArcCatalog, it will consist of six or so files within a directory.

INTRODUCTION TO ARCGIS

ArcGIS is a scalable system of GIS software produced by Environmental Systems Research Institute (Esri). This system contains three different products: ArcGIS for Desktop Basic (formerly ArcView), ArcGIS for Desktop Standard (formerly ArcEditor), and ArcGIS for Desktop Advanced (formerly ArcInfo). **ArcGIS for Desktop Basic** is meant for a general (non-professional) audience. It is the most popular desktop GIS software program and allows the user to conduct data visualization, query and analysis, as well as the ability to create and edit basic geographic features (Esri, 2012). **ArcGIS for**

Desktop Standard includes all the functionality of ArcGIS for Desktop Basic and adds the ability to edit features in a multi-user geodatabase so that multi-user editing and versioning are possible. Standard also adds the ability to edit topologically integrated features in a geodatabase. **ArcGIS for Desktop Advanced** is Esri's professional GIS software. It includes all of the functionality in Standard, and adds some advanced geoprocessing and spatial analysis and data conversion capabilities. Importantly, the user is able to incorporate additional tools and capabilities by adding extensions found on Esri's website (http://www.esri.com/software/arcgis/arcgis-for-desktop/extensions).

INTRODUCTION TO ARCGIS FOR DESKTOP

We will focus on the two main applications found on ArcGIS for Desktop: ArcCatalog and ArcMap. Although they are designed to work together, they run under separate executable files (.exe) and have their own icons.

ArcCatalog works like Windows Explorer. It is a place to browse and manage your data. You can also create and edit metadata in ArcCatalog.

ArcMap is where you actually create maps and analyze spatial data.

INTRODUCTION TO ARCCATALOG

ArcCatalog is designed to help manage your spatial and non-spatial data files.

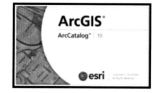

From Windows Taskbar: click the Start menu→ Click "ArcGIS" and select "ArcCatalog 10"

The Geography Toolbar

Both ArcCatalog and ArcMap use a general tool bar for map navigation and query within the active data frame. There are several general toolbar tools and icons that that you should become familiar with. Additional tools located on the toolbar will be discussed in more depth later on.

The **Zoom In / Zoom Out** tools let you click on your map to zoom in or out at a fixed amount or to draw a box around the area that you want to see in more or less detail. The new map will be drawn so that the area you drew the box around is in the middle of the map display.

Think of the **Pan** tool as a sticky hand. Left click on your map display, hold the mouse button down, and move your map. Your extent (amount zoomed in or out) stays the same while your map moves.

The **Full Extent** button will zoom in or out so that all of your active (checked) map layers can be viewed. You can also zoom in to a single layer by right clicking on the layer in the table of contents and choosing "zoom to layer."

Using the **Identify** tool, click on a map feature in the map display. An "identify results" box will display that feature's attribute information. Notice the layers dropdown menu in the identify results box. The default in ArcMap is to display information only about the top-most layer.

  The **Go Back to Previous Extent** button return the map to a previous extent. The **Go to Next Extent** button allows you to jump forward an extent.

BASIC TASKS IN ARCCATALOG

Connecting to Folder

When you launch **ArcCatalog** a list of folders and sub-folders on your computer will be displayed on the left in the catalog tree. "Connect to folder" allows you to make a direct connection to the place on your computer where your GIS data are stored.

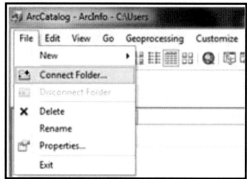

 From the standard toolbar: click "**File**" and then select "**Connect Folder…**" or simply click on the "Connect to Folder" icon (shown above) on the tools toolbar.

Once you launched the Connect to Folder/Connect Folder option, browse to the folder with your data.

Seeing File Types

When the "Contents" tab is active, ArcCatalog will indicate the type of file (e.g., point, line, or polygon) using different icons. In the example to the right, the file "Maritime_Piracy_2009.shp" is made up of point features and "Littoral_Failed_State_Buffer.shp" is made up of polygon features. "Maritime_Piracy_2009_Table.dbf" is a data table.

Previewing Files

By making the "Preview" tab active, you can preview the map features and attribute data. When the preview drop-down menu at the bottom of the window is set to "Geography," you can see

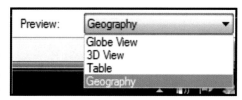

what your geographic data looks like. You need to view your data in ArcMap in order to make changes to the way it displays, but this preview in ArcCatalog allows you to look at it quickly. ArcCatalog may ask you if you want to build pyramids in order to display raster data or other images: Select "Yes". Switch the preview drop-down to "Table" to view the attribute data associated with your geographic features.

  *In the table preview mode, click on the "**Table Options**" button to add a new field or export the table.*

Right clicking on a column heading of the table in preview mode allows you to access a number of other functions such as Sort, Freeze/Unfreeze Column, Delete Field, and Statistics (the statistics option is only available for numeric fields).

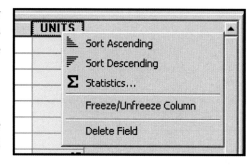

Checking Properties

Double click on the file name to bring up the shapefile table properties (or by right-clicking the file name and choosing "**Properties**" from the menu).

With the "Fields" tab active, you can identify the data type for each of the columns in your table. When you click on a column name, the length of the field will appear. When you click on the field name "Shape," several new field properties appear at the bottom. From the "XY Coordinate System" tab, you can see what datum and projection have been defined (if any). Three coordinate systems are most commonly used: Geographic Coordinate System (GCS), Universal Transverse Mercator (UTM), and State Plane Coordinate (SPC). (For more information about coordinate systems, see Chapter 4). From the "Indexes" tab, you can create attribute or spatial indexes in order to increase the speed of searching, querying, and drawing data.

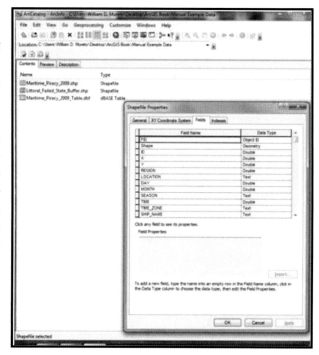

Searching for Map Data

You can search for geographic data on disk or across a network. On the ArcCatalog toolbar, click the Search button. The "Search" dialog box opens with the "ALL" tab active. The tabs on the Search dialog box give you different ways to search for data. On the ALL tab, you search by file name or type. In addition, you can also conduct a narrower search by selecting the "Maps", "Data" and "Tools" tabs.

 You may need to register GIS data folders for indexing before being able to search for it. To do so, simply click on the "Index / Search Options" button, select "Add..." and click the appropriate folder.

INTRODUCTION TO ARCMAP 10

ArcMap is where you create maps and access most of the ArcGIS functionality.

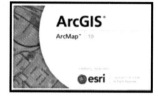

 From Windows Taskbar: Click the Start Menu → Click "ArcGIS" and select "ArcMap 10". **From ArcCatalog:** Click the ArcMap icon.

When ArcMap opens, a default window will open and ask if you want to open an empty map, use a template, or open an existing map. You can prevent this dialog from displaying again by checking the box next to "Do not show this dialog in the future".

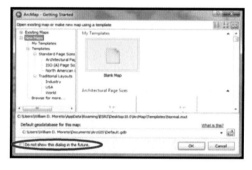

Customizing the Interface

ArcMap is made up of many different windows and (dockable) toolbars that you can resize and move around.

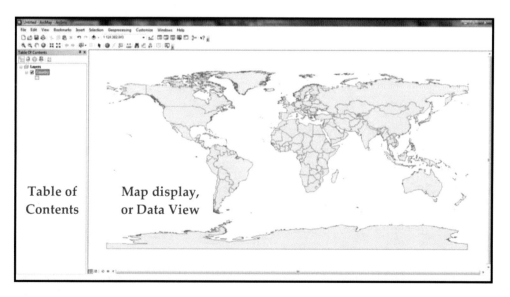

The window that lists your map layers is the Table of Contents (TOC); the window that shows your map is the map display, or Data View. You can close the Table of Contents by clicking on the "x", or resize it by holding the mouse cursor over the right edge until the cursor changes to a two-headed arrow. Left-click the mouse and drag the edge to resize the TOC. To move a toolbar, left-click and hold on the toolbar's end (top or left) and drag to a new location.

Working with the Table of Contents (TOC)

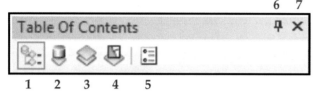

1. **List By Drawing Order:** Display map layers based on order when added to Data Frame.
2. **List By Source:** Maps are categorized and displayed based on where the data was stored.
3. **List By Visibility:** Display map layers based on whether they are currently visible.
4. **List By Selection:** Display selected characteristics of map layers.
5. **Options:** Set options for the TOC.
6. **Auto Hide:** When enabled, TOC is 'hidden' as a tab when not in use.
7. **Close:** Closes the TOC.

Map layers are drawn in the Data View in the order they appear in the Table of Contents. Map layers listed at the top will draw on top of other layers. To move a map layer above or below others, left click and hold the mouse button down, then drag the layer to its new location in the TOC.

The Standard Toolbar

This toolbar typically appears at the top of the ArcMap application window and is used for map printing, creating a new map, opening an existing map, saving your map, starting related ArcGIS applications, and more.

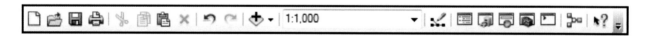

Data Frames

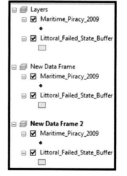

Data frames group map layers in ArcMap's Table of Contents. When you open ArcMap, the default will be one data frame called "Layers". Map layers added to ArcMap become part of this data frame. You may only need one data frame in a map document. But if you need to include more than one map in your layout (including the same map at a different extent), you will need two or more data frames (Also see "Creating Extent Rectangles" in Chapter Three).

 From the Standard Toolbar: click "**Insert**" then select "**Data Frame**".

Adding Data

From the Table of Contents: right-click the data frame you would like to add data to and select "**Add Data…**". **Or,** Click the **"Add Data…"** icon.

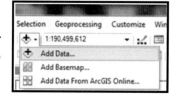

The Add Data button in ArcMap allows you to add an external shapefile or table or to import data from ArcGIS online. For example, the basemap (below) was obtained from *Bing Maps Hybrid* using the "Add Basemap…" option.

Moving or Removing Layers From a Data Frame

Right-click the layer then select "**Copy**". Next, right-click the destination data frame and click "**Paste Layer(s)**". To remove a layer, right-click the layer and select "**Remove**".

Activating a Data Frame

The map layers in only one data frame can be displayed in the Data View at a given time. It does not matter which data frame is listed first in the table of contents; it matters which data frame is "active".

From the Table of Contents: right-click the Data Frame you wish to activate and select "**Activate**".

The Tools Toolbar

1 and 2: The **Fixed Zoom In / Fixed Zoom Out** tools work like the zoom tools. Each time they are clicked, ArcMap zooms in or out a fixed amount.

3 and 4: The **Select Features** tool (3) allows you to select features on the map. The default in ArcMap is to select features on the top-most layer. You are given the option of Selecting by Rectangle, by Polygon, by Lasso, by Circle, or by Line:

> **Selecting by Rectangle:** all features will be selected within a user-defined rectangle.
> **Selecting by Polygon:** all features will be selected within a user-defined polygon.
> **Selecting by Lasso:** all features will be selected within a user-defined shape. Unlike a polygon, the sides of the lasso do not have to geometrically equal.
> **Selecting by Circle:** all features will be selected within a user-defined circular shape.
> **Selecting by Line:** all features will be selected that interest with a user-defined line.

There are several ways you can select features with the **Select Features** tool, such as with your mouse pointer as enabled by the tool. You can also select features in the map by selecting their records in the attribute table or graph window with your mouse pointer. Map features and their respective attributes are simultaneously selected on the map, table, or graph—regardless of where the initial selection originated from. The **Clear Selected Features** tool (4) clears all selected features on an active layer.

5: The **Measure** tool lets you to draw a line, or a series of connected lines, to roughly measure the Euclidean (straight-line, or 'as the crow flies') distance between locations on the map. When you use the Measure tool in snapping mode, it will snap to the vertices of lines and polygons, or to point features. This makes it easy to trace over features, such as to measure the exact distance between street intersections. If you want to snap to edges hold down the "Ctrl" key on your keyboard when measuring.

6: The **Go to XY** tool allows you to enter longitudinal (x) and latitudinal (y) coordinates and navigate to them.

Viewing Attributes of Selected Features

In some cases, you may want to view the selected map features in the map layer's Attributes Table. For example, applying a selection is a way of specifying the specific features for which you want to calculate statistics, view attributes, move, edit, and so on.

From the Table of Contents: Right-click the layer you wish to work with, select "**Open Attribute Table**" and click ▣. **Or, from the Table of Contents**: Right-click the layer you wish to work with and select "**Selection**". Click the "**Open Table Showing Selected Features**". **Or:** Click ▣ after you selected your features *within* the layer attribute table.

Using the Measure Tool

Click on your map at the starting location. Move your cursor to your end location, or next location, and click once. Repeat as needed to measure multiple segments. Double click to finish. ArcMap will display the cumulative distance in the bottom left part of the GUI (below the Table of Contents). If you move the cursor outside of the Data Frame, the distance results will disappear.

 The measure tool will use the display units you specified in the Data Frame Properties (right click on the name of the Data Frame > Properties > "General" tab).

Using the Go to XY Tool

Click on the XY icon to open the "Go to XY" dialog window. The first thing you will notice on the window is a space for you to enter your coordinates: Longitudinal refers to the x-coordinates and latitudinal refers to the y-coordinates.

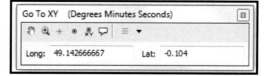

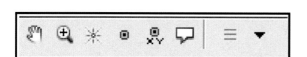

1: Use the **Pan** tool to move the map viewer to the proximity of the entered coordinates.

2: The **Zoom to** tool moves the map view to the proximity of the entered coordinates and also provides an up-close look.

3: The **Flash** tool simply creates a "flash" (temporary) point of the entered coordinates.

4: The **Add point** tool allows you to "permanently" place a point of the entered coordinates within the active layer. This tool allows you to keep the entered point on the map while also entering other coordinates.

5: The **Add labled point** tool does exactly the same thing as the Add point tool, except it also provides the coordinates of the point around the point.

6: The **Add callout** tool provides a call out box with the points coordinates.

7: The **Recent** tool provides a list of all the recent coordinate entries. This allows you to go back and forth from previously entered coordinates.

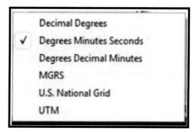

8: The coordinate units you are able to input using the XY tool are listed under the **Units** tool (see right). It is extremely important that you click on this tool and choose the appropriate units you will be using before you enter your coordinates.

ZOOM IN: Mapping Maritime Piracy Incidents With XY Coordinates

Adapted or excerpted directly from Caplan, J.M., Moreto, W.D., & Kennedy, L.M. (2011). Forecasting Global Maritime Piracy Utilizing the Risk Terrain Modeling (RTM) Approach to Spatial Risk Assessment. In L.W. Kennedy and E. F. McGarrell (Eds.) Crime and Terrorism Risk: Studies in Criminology and Criminal Justice. New York, NY: Routledge.

Recent maritime piracy incidents on the coast of Somalia, the Gulf of Aden and the Horn of Africa (HoA) have generated a significant amount of attention from the media, policy strategists and academic researchers. While modern maritime piracy is not a new phenomenon, changes in geographic "hotspots," the increased frequency of incidents, and the severity of attacks warrant that the current maritime piracy situation be assessed. While there has been anecdotal evidence outlining specific geo-spatial and temporal factors that contribute to maritime piracy, there has been no attempt to empirically test how such factors intersect at places to create a context conducive for maritime piracy to occur. Indeed, the identification of the land-based factors that contribute to maritime piracy has been considered a vital topic in need of assessment. But sea-based risk assessments tend to rely on univariate analysis (past incidents) to identify "hotspots." This neglects the dynamic environment (social, natural, etc) in which such incidents occur. This study attempted to address this issue by creating a context-driven risk map of maritime piracy on the Earth's waterways.

The researchers incorporated the Risk Terrain Modeling (RTM; www.riskterrainmodeling.com) approach to spatial risk assessment. The authors conceptualized and operationalized variables that were recognized in empirical research and expert opinions as being relevant to maritime piracy, including shipping routes, maritime chokepoints and state status (as defined by the Failed State Index). However, creating a risk terrain map was only one part of the study. Plotting maritime piracy incidents on a map was also necessary. Fortunately, such information is provided as XY coordinates by the International Maritime Bureau (IMB). The XY tool in ArcGIS was used to map these coordinates of maritime piracy incidents. Although the IMB provided the coordinates in *degrees:minutes:seconds* (dms) format, The XY tool transformed them into the required *decimal degrees* (dd) format and displayed the coordinates as points on a map.

Once the maritime piracy incidents were mapped (2009 incidents were used), they were superimposed onto the risk terrain map layer. According to a logistic regression analysis, for every one unit increase in risk value, the likelihood of a pirate attack increased by 184% (p <.001). A Pearson Chi-squared test showed that the top 10% of high-risk cells in the RTM map correctly forecasted 61% of the maritime piracy incidents in 2009 (p <.01). This is quite a feat considering that pirate attacks only occur in approximately 1.3% of all cells throughout the globe. Overall, the study was a step forward in addressing global maritime piracy by focusing on qualities of space that enable piracy to happen most easily rather than solely on the hotspot locations of past pirate attacks.

Adding Tools and Toolbars

ArcMap provides a variety of tools and toolbars. You may become particularly fond of some. If you use them often, it may be worth your while to add them to your ArcMap interface—for easy access. Anything with a check mark next to it in the Toolbars menu will be displayed in ArcMap. You can also add new buttons to your toolbars from the "Customize Mode…" option. From there, you can add a specific tool—rather than an entire toolbar. To do this, left-click on the tool you want and drag it to an existing toolbar that is already displayed in ArcMap.

 From the Standard Toolbar: click "**Customize**" then select "**Toolbars**".

Showing Map Tips

Map tips are small text boxes that appear when you hold the cursor over a map feature. You can determine which field in your attribute table is used in the map tips. To change the primary data field, make the "Fields" tab active in the "Layer Properties" dialog box and choose a desired field from the "Primary Display Field" dropdown menu.

 From ArcMap: right-click the layer you want to work with and select "**Properties**". Click the "**Display**" tab and check the "**Show Map Tips**" box.

Saving Map Projects

ArcGIS can integrate many different types of data. The most common types are tabular data and geographic data, but you may also use various images. ArcMap can also create additional types of files, including map documents (.mxd) and map layers (.lyr). Naming and storing these files in a consistent manner will make your work with ArcGIS much easier.

 From the Standard Toolbar: click "**File**" then select "**Save As…**".

If you save all of your work in ArcMap, you will create a map document (.mxd). This file will save all of the work you have done, including changes you have made to layer properties, symbology, and the map layout. This .mxd file does NOT save the original data you added as layers to your map. Instead, it includes information about the location of those files on your computer (or network, or Internet) and the formatting changes you made. **This means that you cannot move the data files you have included in a map document without running into problems**. It also means that map projects are difficult to transfer from one computer to another. If you do move one of the files used in your map document, that layer will be shown with a ! next to it and will not draw when you open your project. If you click on the grayed out check mark beside the layer name in the TOC, ArcMap will display a dialog box asking where you moved the file to. Navigating to the file in its new location and clicking "Add" will solve the problem, but this can be time-consuming (and frustrating), so it is best avoided. **Manage your files strategically from the start of your project.**

Relative Paths

One way to minimize problems when you move files that are part of an ArcMap document is to use relative paths. If you specify that you want to use relative paths, ArcView will be able to find the pieces (i.e. different component files) of your ArcMap document if you move them.

 From the standard toolbar: click "**File**", select "**Map Document Properties**" and click the "**Store relative pathnames to data sources**" box.

 You can also provide descriptive information (i.e. title, summary, etc) about the map document from the Map Document Properties.

Saving Map Layers

In addition to saving the entire workspace with a map document, you can save the appearance of an individual map layer. This (.lyr) file will store all the formatting and symbology changes you made to the layer. This is particularly helpful if you want to use the same layer, with the same symbology, in another map document—but do not want to recreate the appearance every time. As with the .mxd file, the .lyr file only includes information about the formatting and the directly path to the original data.

 From the Table of Contents: right-click the map layer you wish to work with and select "**Save As Layer File**".

Naming Files

Giving your files clear and consistent names will make working with ArcGIS much easier. You need to develop your own naming convention that makes sense to you. ArcGIS can work with file names that are more than 8 characters, but really long names can be difficult to view in certain dialog boxes. ArcGIS can also work with files that have spaces in their name, but this will create problems if you work with the Spatial Analyst extension. Your file names should help you distinguish the content and version of your data. To avoid problems, refrain from using spaces or punctuation marks in file or folder names. The underscore character (_) is a good way to separate text without using spaces. Another common naming convention is to begin each word with uppercase letters, and no spaces (e.g., PhilaStreets.shp).

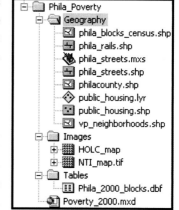

Storing Files

The most important thing in storing files for ArcMap is to think through a system BEFORE you start. Consider creating a new directory for each new mapping project. Keep all map documents in that directory. Create subdirectories for geographic data, images, and tabular data that are not associated with geographic files. Keep map layers in the same directory as the geographic data that they reference.

Geodatabases

Geodatabases allow for topologically integrated features and define rules for the behavior of different types of objects. This provides a much more sophisticated approach to storing and managing data than using directories and subdirectories, and it works well for sharing data.

INTRODUCTION TO ARCGIS DESKTOP HELP

Sooner or later, you will need help with ArcGIS software. ArcGIS Desktop Help is the first place you should turn to get answers to basic technical, functional, and operational questions about ArcGIS applications and related tools. The ArcGIS Desktop Help system contains a navigation pane—with Contents, Favorites and Search tabs—and a topic pane for viewing Help topics. Both panes are visible in the viewer at all times, allowing you to keep track of where you are in the Contents structure of the Help system.

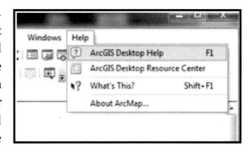

From the Windows Taskbar: Click the Start button then select "**Programs**". Click "**ArcGIS**", select "**ArcGIS Desktop Help**" and click "**ArcGIS 10 Help**". **Or, from ArcMap or ArcCatalog**: Press the "F1" key on your keyboard. **Or:** Click "**Help**" from the standard toolbar in ArcMap or ArcCatalog, then select "**ArcGIS Desktop Help**".

Searching Help for Key Words

If you want to learn how to perform a specific task or if you need more information about a specific concept or tool, it is best to search for Help topics that contain related key words or phrases.

From ArcGIS Desktop Help: click the "**Search**" tab, type in any related key words or phrases and click "**Ask**". Links that are related to your search with appear in order of relevancy. View the desired topic in the topic pane to the right.

⚠ *Use double quotation marks to string together words in the search (e.g. "Buffer Distance").*

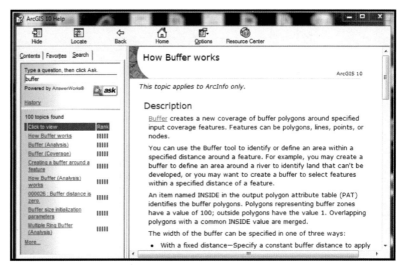

Getting Help Directly Within the Applications

When you position the mouse pointer over a button or menu command, the name of the item appears. A brief description also appears in the status bar at the bottom of the application window.

To get help with a command in a drop-down menu or button in a toolbar, click the "What's This" tool ▸? on the ArcMap or ArcCatalog Standard Toolbar, then click the item you want help with.

To get help with a command in a context menu (i.e., the menu launched by right-clicking), highlight the command and press Shift + F1.

To get help with a control in a dialog box, click the "What's This?" button ▸? at the top of the dialog box and then click the control. On some dialog boxes there are also "About" or "Help" buttons, both of which provide additional information specific to the dialog box.

To get help on a window, such as the Table of Contents or the Identify Results window, click inside the window, then press Shift + F1.

Direct access to the online Help for each tool and toolbox in ArcToolbox is available by using the "Show Help" button—in the tool's dialog box, which provides a general description of the tool and documentation for each parameter.

CHAPTER TWO

Communicating with Maps

MAP SYMBOLOGY

ArcMap has many options for changing the way your data are displayed. To make quick changes, click on the layer symbol under the layer's name in the Table of Contents. The "Symbol Selector" window that opens will look different depending upon the type of layer: point, line, or polygon. For points, you can choose a different marker. When you choose a new marker, the default size jumps to 18 point (quite large). You can change the color, size, and angle using the options on the right side of the "Symbol Selector" window. For lines, the options are similar to point features. For polygons, you have choices about the fill pattern, fill color, and outline color.

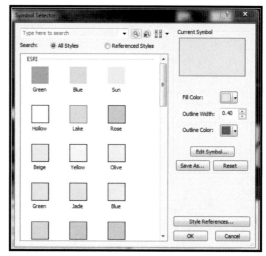

 From the Table of Contents: Right-click the layer you wish to work with, select "**Properties**" then click the "**Symbology**" tab.

 Remove the check mark next to one of the categories of symbols if you find that it is not helpful (to reduce the amount of scrolling necessary to find appropriate symbols).

The "Reset" button in the "Symbol Selector" window will undo any changes you have made to the symbol since opening the window. The "Edit Symbol…" button gives you additional options (often too many options) but may be helpful in fine-tuning the symbol's appearance.

Symbolizing Point Features[12]

Symbolizing features means assigning them colors, markers, sizes, widths, angles, patterns, transparency and other properties by which they can be displayed on a map. Symbols may look like the objects they represent, as when the lake polygon is blue. Or on a street map, varying line thickness may show whether the street is a local road, an arterial, or a highway without implying that the widths on a map are proportional to the widths of the actual streets. By varying simple properties, you can convey information about map features.

Single Symbol

The default in ArcMap is to represent all points with the same size, shape, and color symbol. This is how ArcMap will display your point shapefiles when they are first added to a map document or when you create them through geocoding or adding XY data.

 Open the layer properties by double-clicking on the layer in the TOC or right-click then select "**Properties**". Then click on the "**Symbology**" tab in the "Layer Properties" dialog window. In the box on the left side, "Single Symbol" will be highlighted. You can change the size, shape, and color of the symbol by clicking on it, but as long as "**Single symbol**" is selected, all of your point features will appear the same on the map.

Unique Value

Unique value displays different symbols for points with different attribute values. This can work well for layers with minimal variation in attribute values among features or for layers with only a few points (e.g. 10 or fewer points). This symbology but can quickly be overwhelming for larger files.

From the "**Symbology**" tab of the "Layer Properties" window, click "**Categories**" on the left side. Select the "**Unique Values**" option. You will be able to change the "**Value Field**", which identifies which field from the layer's attribute table will be used to distinguish each feature with a different symbol. After selecting a value field, click the "**Add All Values**" button. ArcMap will list a symbol for "**<all other values>**" that you can remove by taking away the check mark. You can change the individual symbols by clicking on them. You can make changes to all of the symbols, or only some of them: hold down the shift key to select two or more, then right clicking on the values to adjust the symbology properties. To remove a value, right click on it and choose "**Remove Value(s).**" Use the black arrows on the far right to move values up and down (this is the order your values will appear in the legend on your map).

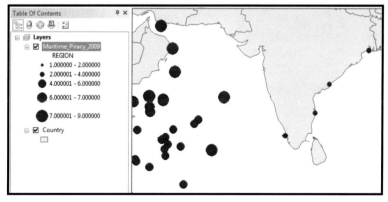

Graduated Symbol

Graduated symbols allow you to have different size symbols to proportionately represent different attribute values of the layer features.

From the "**Symbology**" tab, click "**Quantities**" on the left hand side and select "**Graduated Symbols**". You will be able to change the "**Value Field**", which identifies which field from the layer's attribute table will be used to distinguish each feature with a sized different symbol. In addition to this, you are able to adjust the number of categories. The default is five, meaning that five value ranges are represented by different size dots on the map. Use the "**Classes**" dropdown menu to change the number of categories.

There are many ways to break up value ranges into categories. The default is "Natural Breaks," which uses Jenks optimization to identify grouping of values that minimize within-group differences. To change this, click on the "Classify" button and use the "Method" dropdown menu to choose a different classification system. You can also adjust the cutoff points by moving the blue vertical lines in the histogram that shows the frequency of values. Alternatively, you can change values manually on the previous screen by clicking on them (you will only be able to change the ending value for each category).

CREATE NEW SYMBOLS FROM BITMAP IMAGES[13]

While ArcGIS provides a basic set of fonts (symbols) to use for representing point features, you have the ability to conduct minor edits within the "Symbol Selector" and the "Symbol Property Editor". Once you begin to work with your selected symbol, you can make any necessary edits to the image size, background color, or transparency.

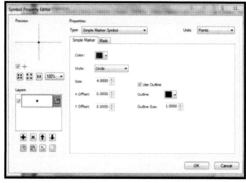

From the Table of Contents: Click on the symbol below the layer name you wish to work with. This opens the "**Symbol Selector**" box. Click the "**Edit Symbol...**" button to open the "**Symbol Property Editor**" window. From there, click the "**Type**" dropdown menu, select the "**Picture Marker Symbol**" and choose the symbol you wish to import. **Or, from the Table of Contents:** Right-click the layer you wish to work with and select "**Properties...**". From the "**Symbology**" tab, click "**Features**" and select "**Single symbol**". Within the "**Symbol**" box, select a symbol to begin working with and to open the "**Symbol Selector**" box. From here, you can refer to the steps of the aforementioned first option beginning with: Click the "**Edit Symbol...**" button...

You are able to create your own symbols in ArcMap by converting any bitmap (.bmp) image. All you need is a basic graphics program that can save images in a bitmap (BMP) file format. The Paint application, which comes standard with Windows Operating Systems software, will suffice. You can draw your own bitmap image or use a pre-existing one (be careful about copyright issues). For example, you might use an image of a school bus to identify locations of school bus stops on a map. If this image is already a bitmap image file, then you can skip to the next step. If it is JPG, GIF, or some other file format, you must first convert it to BMP. To quickly convert a JPG or GIF image to BMP, open it in Windows Paint (usually located in the Start Menu > Accessories). Once opened, save it as a BMP by going to File > Save As. If necessary, you can change the file type in the "Save as type" drop down menu to .bmp.

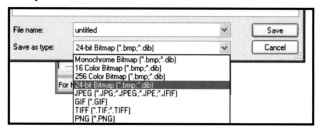

Image-derived symbols can take more time to refresh on a map than basic ArcMap symbology (depending on the size of the image). Therefore, if you have many points, displaying these symbols on a map can take considerable time and may frustrate your other GIS analysis tasks. To avoid this, use basic (i.e. default) symbols in preliminary steps and change to image-derived symbols for your final map layout.

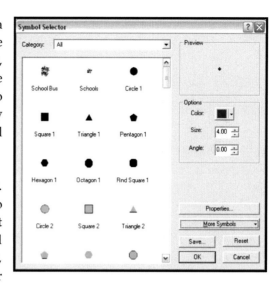

Another word of caution: use picture symbols sparingly. Remember that the purpose of your map is to communicate information. While clever symbols might get the "ooos-and-aaahs", they are not always the best method to impart information. If the symbol is too small, unclear, or difficult to interpret, it could create confusion and/or draw attention away from the main purpose of the map, thereby diminishing its value. People get distracted easily. Furthermore, a "cartoony" (and stereotypical) image of a burglar to represent burglaries may appear unprofessional. Conversely, a handgun to represent shootings or a car to represent auto thefts may reduce the need of the map reader to refer back-and-forth to the legend. Then again, guns could also represent "unlawful possession" or "registered gun permit holders", and cars could represent "traffic accidents" or "carjacking". Pictures do "speak a thousand words", but you do not want them to speak more than your map's legend.

STYLE REFERENCED SYMBOLS

Esri provides templates of symbols for particular purposes, including crime analysis, environmental, business and homeland security.

From the "**Symbol Selector**" window, click the "**Style References…**" button. Click on the empty box beside the style template you wish to use. To set the styles you selected as a default for future use, click the "**Set as Default List…**" button.

SYMBOLIZING POLYGON FEATURES

The symbols in ArcMap can be used for any type of data—points, lines, or polygons. The following symbology schemes work particularly well with polygon features.

Graduated Color

From the "**Layer Properties**" window, select the "**Symbology**" tab then click "**Quantities**". Select the "**Graduated colors**" option and choose the values you wish to reference from the "**Value**" dropdown menu. Use the "**Classes**" dropdown menu and the options in "**Classify**" to change the number of categories or the method for breaking values into exclusive categories. You can normalize a value in order to transform it into a rate using the "**Normalization**" dropdown menu.

For example, in order to show the percent of households receiving public assistance, normalize the total number of households receiving public assistance by the total number of households. (Alternatively, you can create new fields in your attribute table corresponding to rates). Choropleth maps are best used to represent rates rather than raw counts since raw counts can look deceptively high for large polygons. Graduated color communicates information best when you use the same shade of a single color, with lighter shades representing lower values and darker shades representing higher values. But keep in mind that it may be impossible to distinguish between more than four or five shades of the same color, depending upon the quality of your monitor or printer.

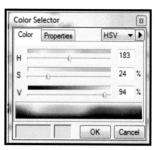

To fine-tune colors, go to "More Colors" when choosing a color from the symbol selector. Here you can play with the hue (H), saturation (S), and value (V); red (R), green (G), and blue (B) and; cyan (C), magenta (M), yellow (Y), and key (black).

Fill Patterns

You can use different patterns in addition to, or instead of, using different colors to represent unique values. Patterns are particularly useful when you are restricted to printing maps in black and white.

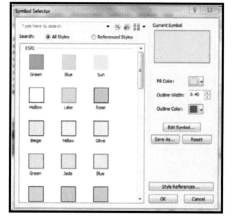

 From the "**Symbology**" Tab of the "Layer Properties" window, choose "**Quantities**" then select "**Graduated Colors**". Select the field with the values you want to display. Set the number of classes and the method of classification. Then double-click on the symbols and change the fill from the "**Symbol selector**" window. Click on the "**Edit Symbol…**" button to fine-tune the fill pattern.

⚠ *Style referenced patterns are also available for fill patterns.*

Dot Density

Dot density maps use randomly placed dots within polygons to represent different values. They are an alternative to choropleth maps to represent raw counts, although it is important to remember (and communicate to anyone reading your map) that the points do not represent precise locations.

 From the "**Symbology**" tab of the "Layer Properties" window, click "**Quantities**" then select "**Dot density**." From "**Field Selection**," choose the field you wish to use as the basis for the map.

Counts (such as the population per square mile) are appropriate for dot density maps, but averages, medians, and rates are not. Choose your dot size, or keep the default (which is advisable, at least to start). The "Min," "Mean," and "Max" boxes will give you a preview of how your map will look. The "**Dot Value**" indicates how many units each dot represents. Change this as needed to create dot densities that have enough dots to show variation but not so many that they are all on top of each other. You can change the color of the dot by clicking on it under "**Symbol**" in the top right part of the screen. Checking "**Maintain Density**" will ensure that the dot density looks the same as you zoom in and out (by making the dots bigger and smaller depending on the map's scale).

Pie Charts

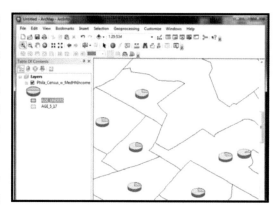

Charts are good for showing multiple values and the relationship among values of different variables. Pie charts are especially good for showing proportions of a whole. For example, individual pie pieces can be used to show the breakdown by age groups for the population in a census tract. Pie charts contain a lot of information, so it can sometimes be difficult to display them clearly on a map.

 From the "**Symbology**" tab of the "Layer Properties" window, click "**Charts**" then select "**Pie**". Holding down the "Ctrl" key on your keyboard, select the fields that you want to include. Make sure that together, they add up to 100 percent (you may need to create and calculate a new field in your attribute table before using charts—so you have appropriate data). Click on the "**Background**" button to change the color or fill ("Hollow" or white backgrounds might be best, so you do not have too many colors in your map). If you check "**Prevent Chart Overlap**", ArcGIS will use "leader lines" to indicate where the pie charts belong if there is no room to display them within the map feature. Click on the "**Properties...**" button to make adjustments to the look of the pie chart (3D, rotation, height). Click on the "**Size...**" button if you want to have different size pie charts depending upon the total (such as total population). If you choose to "**Vary size using a field**," you may need to exclude records with a zero value. To do this, click on the "**Exclusion**" button and, using the appropriate field name, create an expression such as "POP2000=0". You may need to play with the minimum size on the previous screen to make the maximum size pie chart a reasonable size.

Bar/Column Charts

Bar charts can be used to compare values on two or more variables that do not represent proportions (i.e., they do not have to be subsets of a population that add to 100 percent).

From the "**Symbology**" tab in the "Layer Properties" window, click "**Charts**" then select "**Bar/Column**". You are able to select the field(s) you want to work with; the background color; the color scheme; normalization, and whether to prevent chart overlap. To switch from column (vertical) to bar (horizontal) charts, go to "**Properties...**" and select either Bar or Column under "**Orientation**".

Stacked Charts

Stacked charts can be used to compare values on two or more variables (such as gender) that are subsets of a larger variable (such as total population) when you do not know, or do not want to display, all of the subsets. You have many of the same options for formatting (e.g., size, color) that you have with the other types of charts.

CLASSIFICATION SCHEMES

In addition to user-defined ranges for class categories, ArcGIS provides several standard classification scheme options. The four most common classification methods are natural breaks, quantile, equal interval, and standard deviation. If the data are unevenly distributed, with large jumps in values or extreme outliers, and you want to emphasize clusters of observations that have similar values, use the natural breaks classification approach. If the data are evenly distributed and you want to emphasize the percentage of observations in a given classification category or group of categories, use the quantile classification approach. If the data are normally distributed and you want to represent the density of observations around the mean, use the equal interval approach. If the data are skewed and you want to identify extreme outliers or clusters of very high or low values, use the standard deviation classification approach. These classification methods are discussed in more detail below.

The default classification option in ArcGIS is **natural breaks**. In this approach, class categories are identified based on natural groupings in the data. ArcGIS uses a statistical procedure to identify optimal groupings so that values within each class are more similar and values between classes are farther apart. Usually, class breaks are set to correspond with relatively large jumps in the distribution of values. Using natural breaks to classify data tends to be useful when mapping data values that are not evenly distributed, since it places value clusters in the same class.

- The disadvantage of using this approach is that it is often difficult to make comparisons between maps since the classification scheme used is unique to each data set.

The **quantile** classification method assigns an equal number of areas to each class. This method arranges all observations from low to high and assigns equal numbers of observations to each classification category. Thus, if 160 census tracts and four classes exist, then each class grouping contains 40 census tracts, with the lowest 40 in the first group and the highest 40 in the last group. This approach is useful when the data values are fairly evenly distributed or when a need exists to highlight a proportion of the observations.

- The disadvantage in using this approach, especially with positively skewed data, is that differences between classes may be exaggerated since a few widely ranging adjacent values may be grouped together in one class while an equal number of relatively homogeneous values may be grouped together in another class.

The **equal interval** approach divides the distribution of values so that the range of values within each class is identical. In other words, the difference between the highest and lowest value is the same for each class grouping. This approach is useful when data are normally distributed and you are interested in emphasizing observations around the mean. When the objective is to emphasize outliers with high crime rates or hot spot clusters, this could be a useful approach to classifying and mapping the data.

- The disadvantage in using this method with positively skewed data is that most observations will be assigned to the lower value categories and only a few observations will be assigned to the higher value categories.

With the **standard deviation** approach, class breaks are defined by standard deviational distances from the mean. With positively skewed distributions, outliers and hot spot clusters can easily be isolated and identified.

- The disadvantage in using this approach is that the map does not show the actual values in each class, only how far each class category is from the mean.

ADJUSTING TRANSPARENCY

 From the Table of Contents: right-click the map layer you wish to adjust, click "**Properties...**" then select the "**Display**" tab. Adjust the transparency value (%) in the "**Transparency**" text box.

QUERYING GIS DATA

In ArcGIS you can identify a subset of map features based on their attributes or their location. You may use queries as an intermediary step, as part of getting to know your data, to create new values, or to answer your research questions.

Select by Attribute

 From the Standard toolbar: click "**Selection**" then select "**Select By Attributes...**". Your first step in the "Select By Attributes" dialog box is to select a map layer that you want to query (attribute queries are limited to a single layer). In the "**Method**" drop down menu, you need to decide whether you are building on a previous query or starting fresh. In the query dialog box, build an expression using the field names and arithmetic functions or logic operators such as "AND" or "OR". The values associated with each field will be displayed in the text box at the far right. You can use these or type in your own. Click "**Verify**" to make sure ArcMap likes your expression (i.e., formula). You can import (via "Load" button) and save (via "Save" button) expressions. You can also copy and paste text from (or into) the query dialog box using Ctrl + C (copy) and Ctrl + V (paste), respectively,  on your keyboard. When you click the "Apply" button, the map features that satisfy your query will be highlighted with a bright blue outline.

⚠ *If the values you input are text (not numbers), then you must put single quotes around them (e.g. 'Main').*

To review the selected records, right click on the map layer and go to "**Open Attribute Table**." Click on the "Select" button at the bottom to view only the selected records. You can calculate values on an existing or new field for only the selected records (for example, calculating the percent of males to females in block groups with non-zero populations). You can also generate summary statistics for only the selected records by right clicking on a column name in the attribute table and selecting "**Statistics**." To see all of the selected records at the closest extent in the Data Frame, click "**Zoom to Selected Records**" from the "Selection" menu in the Standard Toolbar.

 *You can create a new shapefile from an existing map layer that only includes the selected map features. To do this, right click on the layer (with selected features) in the Table of Contents, select "**Data**" then "**Export Data**." Choose the radio button regarding coordinate systems (you will probably want the default). Choose "Selected Records" in the "Export" drop down menu to create a new shapefile with only the selected features/records.*

Select by Location

The ability to query based on the location of map features is something unique to GIS, and combining attribute and location queries really takes advantage of GIS functionality.

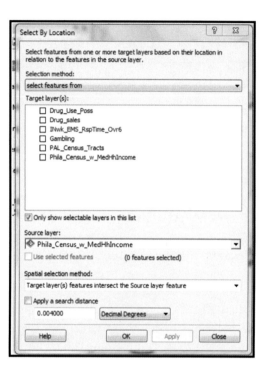

From the Standard toolbar: click "**Selection**" then select "**Select By Location...**"

Your first choice in the "Select By Location" dialog window involves the method of the selection. Are you starting from scratch or querying a subset of map features already selected? In the "Target layers" box, put a check mark next to the map layer(s) whose features you wish to select. The "**Spatial selection method**" drop down menu provides various relationships between the features in target layer and the source layer. The options/images at the bottom of the "Select by Location" dialog window change as you choose different types of relationships between the target and source layers, such as whether you are able to "**Apply a search distance**".

Combining Attribute and Location Queries

The "Select By Attribute" and "Select By Location" functions do not allow you to mix the type of query at the same time. But by performing one type of query first and then conducting a subsequent query on the selected records, you can perform attribute and location queries on the same map layer. For example, you may be interested in what census tracts are located along a river, but you are only interested in census tracts that have at least 100 people living in them. It does not matter which query you do first. Just be sure that the selection method you choose for the second query allows you to add, remove, or select (as appropriate) from the records already selected from the first query.

REMOVING THE SELECTION OF FEATURES OR ATTRIBUTES

From the Standard toolbar: Click "**Selection**" and select "**Clear Selected Features**". Or, from the Table of Contents: Right-click the layer with selected features, click "**Selection**" then click "**Clear Selected Features**".

CHAPTER THREE

Map Design and Layout

LABELING FEATURES

In order to label features manually, you need to activate the "Draw" toolbar.

 From the Standard Toolbar: click "**Customize**", select "**Toolbars**" then click "**Draw**".

Draw Toolbar

The draw toolbar provides several useful tools for labeling specific features and drawing graphics on your map.

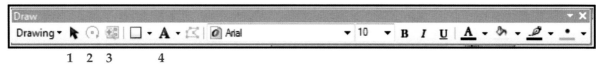

1 2 3   4

1: The **Select Elements** tool allows you to select and move text (e.g., labels) and graphic elements. Also, by double-clicking these elements, their "Properties" box will appear enabling you to change their format (e.g. size, color, font – using the "Change Symbol…" button).

2: Use the **Rotate** tool to manually adjust the position of the text or graphic elements.

3: Use the **Zoom to Selected Elements tool** to zoom to the selected text or graphic.

4: Provides a list of Draw tools. There is no standard name for this as the current selected tool will appear.

Using Draw Tools to Create Text Label Features

 You can place text on a map in order to label map features. There are a few ways to label features on your map:

The "**New Text**" option is the most basic option. It allows you to place text anywhere on your map in a simple text box. The size of the text box is determined by the length of your text.

 Click on the "**New Text**" tool, then click on where you wish to have your text. Hit the '**Enter**' key on your keyboard or click outside of the textbox to finish.

The "**Splined Text**" option allows you to write text along a curved line. This works well for labeling rivers and curvy roads.

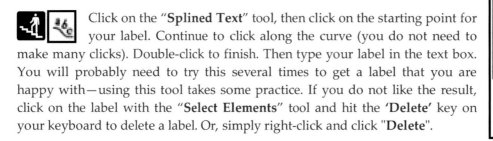 Click on the "**Splined Text**" tool, then click on the starting point for your label. Continue to click along the curve (you do not need to make many clicks). Double-click to finish. Then type your label in the text box. You will probably need to try this several times to get a label that you are happy with—using this tool takes some practice. If you do not like the result, click on the label with the "**Select Elements**" tool and hit the '**Delete**' key on your keyboard to delete a label. Or, simply right-click and click "**Delete**".

The "**Callout**" text tool allows you to place your text away from the map feature while still indicating what is being labeled.

  Using the "**Callout**" tool, click the area where you want the callout box to originate from. To determine the length of the callout box, continue holding down your mouse clicker and release until you are satisfied with the length. If you accidentally release too early or drag out too long, do not worry. You are able to change the length of the callout simply by clicking and holding on the box, then dragging it to a new location.

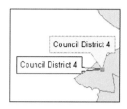

You can draw a polygon-shaped text box using the "**Polygon Text**" option.

  Click the "**Polygon Text**" tool then click on the map where you wish to begin your polygon. Continue creating vertices of your soon-to-be polygon by clicking on your map. Double-click the last location to close the polygon and begin entering text.

The "**Rectangle Text**" and "**Circle Text**" options allow you to create a rectangular or circular text box.

   Using either the "**Rectangle Text**" or the "**Circle Text**" tool, click on the map where you wish to create your text rectangle or circle. Click and hold the mouse to create the desired size of the rectangle or circle and release when satisfied.

 *To edit the text or text box once it is created, double-click it to open the "**Properties**".*

Manually Placing Labels

By manually placing labels, you avoid having your labels act as a group, making it is easier to move or edit a single label. Before you can use the label tools in ArcMap, you need to indicate which field in the attribute table of your map layer you want to use as the basis for labels.

 Right-click the layer you wish to work with, select "**Properties**" then click on the "**Labels**" tab. Leave the "**Label features in this layer**" box unchecked. Choose the appropriate field from the "**Label Field**" dropdown menu. Click on "**Symbol...**" to change the size, style, or font for your labels. (Guessing what size to make your labels is difficult and you will probably need to make small adjustments after seeing what works). Using the "**Placement Properties...**" button, you can instruct ArcGIS what to do about duplicate labels. The "**Scale Range...**" allows you to instruct ArcGIS when to draw or not draw labels, depending on the extent. In order to do this, you need to know the exact scales you will be using (so you will probably just want to leave this alone). The "**Label Styles...**" button gives you access to some fancier label options. The highway labels are particularly helpful.

Once you have established the parameters for your labels, you can begin manually labeling your map features. Using the "Label" tool rather than the text tools allows you to use the values in a layer's attribute table as text for the labels (in other words, you do not have to type the label text as you do with the text tools).

 Click the "**Draw**" tool options button (the "A" button on the "Draw" toolbar) and choose "**Label**". The "**Label Tool Options**" window will open and include "**Placement**" and "**Label Style**" options. For placement, you can either have ArcMap decide where to best position labels or you can do it yourself. For label style, you can either go with the properties set in the "Labels" tab of the layer's "Properties" window or you can choose fancier, predetermined styles. You can move manually placed labels (using the "**Select Elements**" tool) and change their size and style (i.e., double-click the label to bring up "**Properties**"). You can delete a label by clicking on it and pressing the "Delete" key on your keyboard.

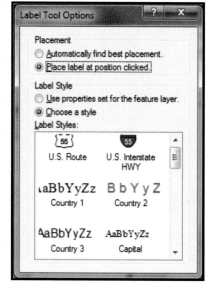

Auto Labeling

You may find it easier to automatically label all of your features. This saves time if you are happy with the way the labels look, but it offers you much less control over the label placement. When you automatically label features, the labels are "dynamic" so changes you make to one (e.g. changing the style) are made to all. To delete your labels, you will need to remove the check mark from "Label Features in this layer" box or re-select "Label Features".

 From the Table of Contents in ArcMap: Right-click the layer you wish to work with, then click "**Properties…**", select "**Labels**" then check the "**Label features in this layer**". Or, from the TOC: Right-click the layer you wish to work with, then select "**Label Features**". To remove labels, either uncheck "**Label features in this layer**" or unselect "**Label Features**".

Converting Labels to Annotation

Labels are one option for placing text on a map. Labels are positioned on the map by the software based on a set of labeling properties defined in the "Labels" tab of the "Layer Properties" dialog box. If you want full control over where labels are placed, you must convert them to annotation.

 From the Table of Contents: right-click the layer after labeling it, then select "**Convert Labels to Annotation…**".

Using Annotation Layers

After labels have been converted to annotation, the annotation class (layer) is automatically added to the map. Annotation groups are listed in the Data Frame Properties dialog box on the Annotation Groups tab.

 From the Table of Contents: right-click the data frame you wish to work with, click "**Properties**" and select the "**Annotation Groups**" tab. Annotation labels can be toggled on or off, and their properties can be changed in this dialog box. Click your desired group then click the "**Properties…**" button. Click the "**Associated Layer**" drop-down list and click <None>. This allows you to turn the annotation layer on and off independently from the map layer.

DESIGNING MAP LAYOUTS

Displaying data so that you can analyze spatial patterns on a computer screen is one thing; printing out a map for other people to look at is another. ArcMap thinks of these as distinct functions and makes available a series of tools for designing map layouts that you do not need until you are ready to publish or print a final map. ArcMap opens in the "Data View", where you use the "Tools" toolbar to navigate your map. When you switch to the "Layout View", you have access to a different range of tools and will use the "Layout" toolbar to navigate. In Layout View, you get a much better idea of how your final map will look when it is printed.

Layout View

 From the Standard toolbar: Click "**View**" then select "**Layout View**". Or, from the ArcMap interface: Click the "**Layout View**" button.

ArcMap will automatically place a border ("neat line") around your map. You can change this by right clicking on it and going to "Properties." Click on the "Frame" tab. From here you can choose a different style or color frame (to get rid of it altogether, choose "no color" from the color selector). You can also change the background color and add a shadow (to add a shadow, you'll need to change the X and Y offset to something other than 0).

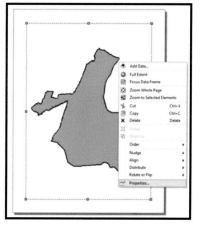

To make your map larger or smaller on the page, you can use the zoom tools on the Tools toolbar or on the **Layout toolbar**. The Layout toolbar also includes a pan tool that you can use to move your whole layout. To move just your map (and not the whole page), use the pan tool in the Tools toolbar. The fixed zoom tools in the Layout toolbar work like the ones on the Tools toolbar. The "Zoom Whole Page" button ⊞ is especially useful.

One of the biggest differences in the Layout View (compared to Data View) is that many more options in the "**Insert**" menu on the Standard toolbar become active. These options allow you to add elements—including a title, legend, north arrow, scale bar, and image—to your layout. Each of these elements will be separate objects in your page layout that can be moved and resized through their Properties. You will not see any of them if you switch back to Data View since they are only meant to be cartographic elements on printed maps. You can add text in the Layout View, but you are better off trying to label features from the Data View, using the label or text tools.

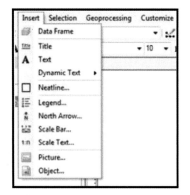

Layout Toolbar →

Tools Toolbar →

Page and Print Setup

By default, the paper size in Layout View is 8.5" x 11", portrait orientation. Make adjustments to the paper size, orientation, and margins, or add page guides from the "Page and Print Setup" dialog box. Guide lines are very helpful for aligning map elements, which can be forced to "snap to guides" to ensure proper and consistent alignment. The paper size, not the data frame's size, dictates the size of the image (i.e. JPG) that will be exported.

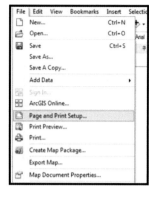 

 From the ArcMap interface: click "**File**" and select "**Page and Print Setup...**"

Adding a Title

 From ArcMap's Layout view: click "**Insert**" on the Standard toolbox and select "**Title**". Type your title in the text box and hit the '**Enter**' key on your keyboard or click the cursor outside the text box. Double-click on the title to bring up the Properties where you can make formatting changes.

Adding and Modifying a Legend

Unless the labels are able to fully explain the map's features and symbology, you will need a legend. ArcMap gives you flexibility in formatting your legend. Your first choice in the "**Legend Wizard**" is what map layers to include. ArcGIS will guess that you want to include all active layers.

From ArcMap's Layout view: click "**Insert**" on the Standard toolbox and select "**Legend...**".

To remove a layer from the legend, click on its name on the right side of the Legend Wizard dialog box and click on the "<" button. The order your layers are listed under "**Legend Items**" will correspond to the order in which they appear in your legend. To change the order, click on the layer name in the "Legend Items" area of the "Legend Wizard" window and hit the up or down arrows (don't worry; this will now affect the order the layers features are drawn). If you want more than one column in your legend, make the adjustment. To see what your legend will look like (before working your way through the rest of the screens), click the "**Preview**" button. If you are satisfied with it, you can click the Finish button and skip the other steps. Otherwise, click the "Preview" button again and click "Next" to continue preparing a legend.

You can change the "**Legend Properties**" of your legend after its been added to the map layout (Right-click on the legend, then select "Properties"). From the Properties window, you can change the title of your legend (or just leave it blank). You can also change the arrangement of your layers ("Items"); add a border, background or drop shadow; or change the size and position of the legend.

 To change the properties of your map once you've closed the "**Legend Wizard**", just double-click your legend.

Adding a Scale Bar

The scale bar is a vital part of any map. Before creating a scale bar, you should determine the units of your map (i.e., feet, kilometers, miles). Once you have determined your map and display units, you can create and insert your scale bar (or scale text—see below).

 From ArcMap's Data view: right-click the layer you wish to work with, click "**Properties…**" and select the "**General**" tab. Within the "**Units**" option, you are able to determine the original map units and the display map units.

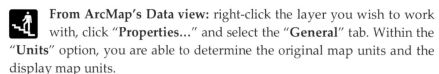 In the "Units" area of the "General" tab of the "Data Frame Properties" window, ArcMap provides a useful tip for additional options for displaying coordinates in the status bar of the ArcMap GUI.

From ArcMap's Layout view: click "**Insert**" on the Standard toolbar and select "**Scale Bar…**". The "**Scale Bar Selector**" window will appear. Select a scale bar to your liking and then click the "**Properties…**" button. You are able to change several attributes of the scale bar, including the number of divisions, subdivisions, frequency of numbers and marks, and the format. You may also change the units of the scale bar. If you wish to change the properties of the scale bar once it is added to the map layout, double-click the scale bar to open the "Scale Bar Selector" window.

Adding Scale Text

You may wish to include a text description of the map scale (i.e., 1 inch = 10 miles).

From ArcMap's Layout view: click "**Insert**" on the Standard toolbar and select "**Scale Text…**". To make changes to or format the units of the scale text, double-click the text that was added to the page layout to open the "**Properties**".

Adding a North Arrow

The north arrow is an important part of any map. Placing a north arrow for a map that depicts the whole world may not be necessary since most people have seen a map of the world and know that North is "up". However, local extents may require a North arrow to prevent confusing an unfamiliar audience.

From ArcMap's Layout view: click "**Insert**" on the Standard toolbar and select "**North Arrow…**". The "**North Arrow Selector**" window will appear. Choose the arrow style. You can manually move the north arrow once added to the map layout. You can also change its properties by double-clicking it.

MAP TEMPLATES

Using map templates can save you time and lead to greater consistency in your published/printed maps. You can use ArcMap's custom templates or design your own. When you open a template, ArcMap starts a new, untitled project with any layout elements or data that was saved in the template. Some templates provided by Esri include (projected) base layer shapefiles.

Opening Map Templates

Decide if you are going to use a map template before you start adding data to your map document. When you open ArcMap, choose to start using ArcMap by clicking on the template radio button in the startup dialog box. The templates listed in the Industry tabs provide empty layouts while those in USA and World tabs include base map layers. Choose a template by double clicking on its name or clicking once and clicking the "OK" button. Do not worry if the template includes colors or elements that you do not want. This is only a starting place for your project that you can customize as needed.

From the Standard toolbar: click "**File**" and select "**New…**".

Using Map Templates

If you selected a map template that contains no data, you must add one or more data layers to your map document. Once you do, the legend and other elements of your layout will be automatically created based on the template design. Make changes to the data frame, legend, scale bar, and north arrow from the Properties dialog boxes (right click on any of these and go to Properties). You can also move the elements around (click and hold down to drag) as needed. Notice that when you use map templates, ArcMap opens in Layout View. You can still switch back (and forth) to Data View using the  buttons.

Using Inset Map Templates

For map templates that include insets, you need to add at least two map layers. When you open one of these templates, you will see Layers 1 and Layers 2 listed in the Table of Contents. By having two separate groups (i.e. Data Frames) of layers, you can have two maps in your page layout. For example, this could be two different map layers or the same map at different extents.

Right-click on the first Data Frame in the TOC and click "**Add Data**…" to select the map layer for the main map in your page layout. Then right-click on the second Data Frame, select "**Add Data**…", and select the map layer for the inset map.

CREATING EXTENT RECTANGLES (INSET MAPS)

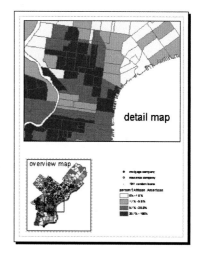

You may need to create a map layout that includes more than one map, either because you cannot fit everything (such as Alaska and Hawaii) on your main map or because you want to zoom into a small area for your main map and indicate on a smaller map what area that covers. Extent rectangles show the extent of one data frame within another data frame. They are dynamic: if you change the extent of either data frame the extent rectangle will update automatically. Extent rectangles also update when the data is rotated or when the projection is changed.

To create an extent rectangle, start with at least two Data Frames: a detail layer and an overview layer (See "Data Frames" section in Chapter One). At least one data frame must be showing an extent that is completely within the extent of the other.

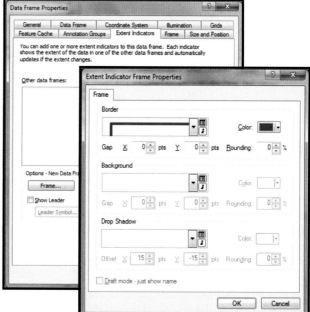

From the Table of Contents: right-click on the data frame that will be receiving the extent rectangle (the overview layer) and select "**Properties**…". From the "Data Frame Properties" dialog window, click the "**Extent Indicators**" tab. Click the data frame with the smaller extent within the "**Other data frames**" column to select it. Click the ">" button to move the selected data frame from the left to the right side—to the "**Show extent indicator for these data frames**" column. Click on the "**Frame**…" button to make changes to the outline of your box. If you wish to have a line distinguish between the smaller and larger extent, click the "**Show Leader**" option.

⚠ *When you have several data frames in a map, name them clearly and descriptively so it is easier to know which to choose when creating an extent rectangle.*

EXPORTING MAPS

If you just need paper copies of your maps, you will probably have the best results printing them from ArcMap. But if you need to insert maps into PowerPoint or word processing files, export the maps as images. You can export a map from ArcMap when you are in Data View or Layout View. However, if you want your exported map to include titles, legends, scale bars, north arrows, and anything else you added to the layout, you need to export from Layout View. There are many options for export formats in the "Save as type" drop down menu.

.PDF — The .pdf format allows you to open the map directly (without inserting it into PowerPoint or MS Word) as long as you have Adobe Reader. This is probably the best option if you need to send someone a map or post a map on the Internet.

.JPG and .PNG — The .jpg format will compromise the quality of your image, so be sure to click on the "options" button when you export and increase the resolution to at least 200 dpi. The .jpg format is good because it stores your map in a fairly small file that will not be compromised if opened on a computer without ArcGIS installed. PNG file sizes tend to be larger, but they do not lose quality during editing.

.TIF and .EPS — The .tif and .eps formats work well if you are going to open your maps in a graphics software package, but they result in larger files.

Screen Capture — If all else fails, you can take a screen capture ("Print Screen" or "Prnt Scrn" key on your keyboard) and then crop the image, but this will not result in a presentation-quality map image.

 From the Standard toolbar: click "**File**" and select "**Export Map…**".

GUIDELINES FOR PROFESSIONAL MAP PRODUCTION[14]

Map Communicability: The intended purpose of the map should be clear and the map should clearly and prominently display the information that is intended to be imparted to the map reader.

Map Layout & Design: Maps should be refined and aesthetically pleasing. Use a consistent layout and cartographic element styles across multiple but related maps. This lets the reader focus on changes to the maps' key features and to make comparisons more easily across multiple maps. Layers should be arranged with key features on top. Be sure that the map and its features are of adequate size, but not too large. You don't want maps to appear too crowded or confusing.

Map Titles and Text: A title and/or subtitle should always be present and should communicate the main purpose of the map. Make sure they suggest what your symbology and category labels actually show. Text should be of adequate size and a very legible font. Text is symbology too. Different text sizes could imply differential importance (i.e. not simply that you are trying to fit the text within a polygon). Space on the map layout is precious, so there is no need to repeat the same text or phrases over again. Text should be clear and concise. Strictly limit your use of abbreviations in order to prevent confusion; some abbreviations mean different things to different people. Proofread your maps for "floating" or unassigned labels and spelling/grammatical errors.

Map Colors: Use as much color contrast as possible between categories, especially with grayscale. For example, with 3 categories, use white, gray and black—not light gray, medium gray, and dark gray. Darker colors commonly represent higher values (or greater significance), and lighter colors represent lower values (or lesser significance). When you reverse this, you risk misinterpretation by your map reader. Consider the photocopy-ability of your map. Color contrasts are greatly diminished when printed or copied in black and white or grayscale. Be sure that all map features are easily distinguishable. Check out ColorBrewer, a web tool for selecting color schemes for thematic maps: http://www.personal.psu.edu/cab38/ColorBrewer/ColorBrewer.html

Symbology: Never use "selection" as symbology. Be sure that map features are identified <u>and</u> map symbology is explained (i.e. polygons represent blockgroups; shading of polygons shows % of population below poverty). Use meaningful class breaks.

Cartographic Elements: Maps should include all necessary (audience appropriate) cartographic elements, including a North arrow and scale bar. Values on a scale bar should be easily additive, divisible, etc.; units should be stated; numbers should not be cluttered. Most visible features on the map should be included in a legend, with few exceptions. However, all items included on a legend should always be visible on the map. Be sure to change the layer/label names from their defaults. Clearly and meaningfully label class breaks and do not include unnecessary decimal places.

INSERTING MAPS INTO MICROSOFT WORD AND POWERPOINT

Start by saving your map as a .jpg in ArcMap. You are probably better off creating map titles in PowerPoint rather than ArcMap. Also, if you are making a map specifically for PowerPoint, consider making the legend larger than usual (14 points or more) so that your audience can read it.

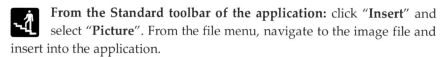  **From the Standard toolbar of the application:** click "**Insert**" and select "**Picture**". From the file menu, navigate to the image file and insert into the application.

You may encounter problems exporting maps to PowerPoint if you try to show the PowerPoint presentation on another computer and it does not have ArcGIS loaded. Your markers (the dots and squares used to represent points on your map) may come up looking like # and other strange symbols. This is because your exported maps are relying on the Esri typefaces to draw these markers correctly. If ArcGIS is not loaded, those typefaces are not available and PowerPoint comes up with the closest approximation from other typefaces. If you use .pdf files or screen captures you can avoid the problem but will sacrifice image quality and flexibility. The other option is to embed all document fonts in the exported map image.

To embed fonts/symbols in map images: When you export maps from the "Layout" view of ArcMap, at the bottom of the Export window, there will be an "Options" button with a down arrow. When you expand these options, there will be three tabs—"General", "Format", and "Advanced." On the "**Format**" tab, check "**Embed all document fonts**".

Picture Toolbar

The "Picture" toolbar provides several tools that let you edit and format images in Microsoft Office applications such as Word or PowerPoint.

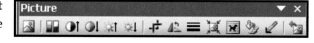

To activate the "Picture" toolbar from within Microsoft Office applications (if it is not already available) go to "**View**" on the Standard toolbar, click "**Toolbars**" and select "**Picture**".

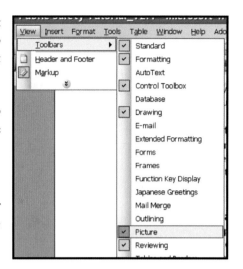

⚠ *The picture toolbar is only visible when a picture is selected. So if you do not see it, be sure a picture in your document is selected (i.e. click on it with your mouse).*

Cropping Map Images

You may notice that there is a lot of white space around your map. Eliminate this in MS Word or PowerPoint by using the "Crop" tool ⌖ on the "Picture" toolbar.

Picture Format and Layout

Formatting the picture by "Wrapping" text around maps, for example, is useful when writing reports.

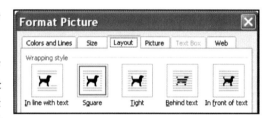

 Click the "**Text Wrapping**" tool on the "**Picture**" toolbar. **Or:** Right-click the image, click "**Format Picture**" then select the "**Layout**" tab. You can also add/edit the image border, size, and alignment from the "Format Picture" dialog window.

PORTABLE DOCUMENT FORMAT (PDF) FILES

Portable Document Format, or PDF, is a digital file format created by Adobe Systems for document exchange in a manner that is independent of the original software application. PDF files are an excellent way to distribute documents via email or online because they are generally small in file size and can be universally viewed; no matter what computer operating system you open them on, they will look exactly the same. PDF files can be thought of as static images of the original document's content.

Viewing PDF Documents

Adobe Reader is necessary to view PDF files. Many computers already come with this software installed. However, if your computer does not have Adobe Reader installed, you can download it for free at www.adobe.com. It is compatible with most operating systems including PC and MAC. To open a PDF file, click (or double click) it and Adobe Reader will open automatically to display the document.

Saving Maps and Documents as PDF

ArcMap has built-in capability to save map layouts as PDF.

 From the Standard toolbar: click "**File**" then select "**Export Map...**". Within the "Export Map" window, select "PDF" in the "**Save as type**" drop down menu.

This file type is useful if you intend your map layout to be the final product or deliverable. However, it is more likely that you will produce maps in ArcMap, export them as a PDF, JPG, or other image file, and then import them into a Word Document, PowerPoint Presentation, or other software application where you will produce the final document.

The most common (and easiest) way to turn a document into the PDF format is from within the software application where you created the document. For example, convert a Microsoft Word document to a PDF file from within the Microsoft Word application. A "PDF creator" is required to do this. Adobe's software suite for creating and editing PDF files is not freely available and can be expensive. If you do not have Adobe, you will need another PDF creator.

There are several free PDF creators that serve as alternatives to Adobe. "doPDF", for example, is free for both personal and commercial use and permits users to create high-quality searchable PDF files by simply selecting the "Print" command from any application. Because the availability of PDF creators changes constantly, it would be inappropriate to list all of the current options here. Rather, search for "PDF Creator" on www.download.com or another reputable software website for freeware, try-ware, or paid software that creates PDF files and that meets your specific needs.

With PDF creator software installed on your computer, it is likely that you will be able to convert a document to PDF by going to File > Print, and then selecting the PDF Creator from the printer "name" pull-down menu in the "Print" dialog box. Click the "OK" button; you will likely be instructed to choose a file name and directory to store the PDF file.

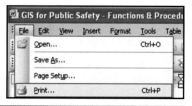

Rather than printing to printer hardware, your document will be "printed", or "imaged," to a new digital PDF file stored on your disk drive.

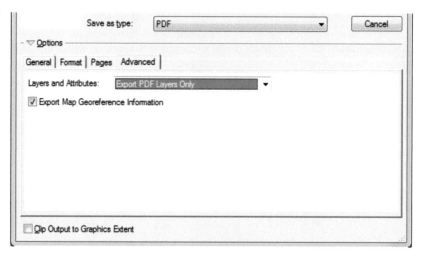

⚠ *When Exporting to a PDF file from ArcMap, it may be useful to view the "Advanced" tab and check the "Export Map Georeference Information (along with Export PDF Layers and/or Feature Attributes). This can be helpful for someone who later opens the PDF and discovers they can display XY coordinates and other map information in the PDF.*

CHAPTER FOUR

Spatial Data and Map Projections

BASE MAPS

Base maps are reference layers for orienting and analyzing primary study data. Typically, they comprise a street centerline and a geographic backdrop such as a census tract, ZIP Code, and/or county boundary. Street centerlines of almost every city, state, or region can be downloaded free from the Internet (see "FREE GIS Data Sources" section).

City planning departments also have GIS data (such as updated street files) that they may be willing to share. You can also integrate data from other sources, such as criminal justice data or health and social services data. Remember, you want to obtain "shapefiles" if possible, which are the most compatible forms of data for use in a GIS. If shapefiles are not already available that's OK. You can create them. But, the data—whether it is your own or from another agency—must have a geographic reference such as street addresses or XY coordinates that can be used to link it to a map.

Examples of criminal justice data include: Number of crime incidents; Types of crime incidents; Locations of police stations, substations, and patrols; Computer-aided dispatch calls; Firearms purchases; Locations of prisons and jails; Locations of criminal and juvenile courts; Open-air drug markets; Gang locations; Jurisdictional lines for state police, county sheriffs, tribal police, and municipal police; Number of protective or restraining orders

Examples of health, social and environmental data include: Locations of public assistance agencies; Locations of public housing; Locations of hospitals and emergency rooms; Locations of mental health programs; Locations of youth shelters; Census data; Neighborhood boundaries; State, county, and Indian Country boundaries; School locations; Business locations; Transportation routes; Park and recreation area

SOME FREE GIS DATA SOURCES

- Criminal Justice Web Sites | http://www.icpsr.umich.edu/icpsrweb/ICPSR
- National Archive of Criminal Justice Data | http://www.icpsr.umich.edu/NACJD/gis
- New Jersey Department of Environmental Protection | www.nj.gov/dep/gis/lists.html
- State of Florida Shapefiles | http://www.fgdl.org
- State of Massachusetts Shapefiles | http://www.mass.gov/mgis/laylist.htm
- Census TIGER/Line® Data | http://www.census.gov/geo/www/tiger/tgrshp2010/tgrshp2010.html
- Geospatial One Stop | http://geo.data.gov/geoportal/catalog/main/home.page
- MapCruzin | http://www.mapcruzin.com

AERIAL PHOTOGRAPHS AND ORTHOPHOTOGRAPHY

Aerial photography refers to photographs of the ground taken from an elevated position. Some of the first aerial imagery of the Earth were hand drawn sketches from hot air balloons. Today, there are much more sophisticated means of acquiring images of our environments, such as with aircraft-mounted gyro-stabilized digital cameras. If you ever used Google® Earth, then you have seen aerial photographs. Digital orthophotography combines the image characteristics of a photograph with the geometric qualities of a map. This is done through a process which converts an aerial photograph to a digital product that has been rectified for camera lens distortion, vertical displacement caused by terrain relief and variations in aircraft altitude and orientation. Digital images such as aerial photographs or orthophotos can be added to ArcMap as a layer—in the same manner as you would add a shapefile. These layers can serve a variety of purposes such as a reference tool for revision of street networks or as a backdrop that provides additional environmental context to shapefile features layered on top. Some state agencies provide aerial photographs to the public via free internet download. *NOTE: Georectifying the images in ArcMap may be necessary.*

ZOOM IN: Police Officers' Perceptions of Maps and Aerial Photos

Adapted or excerpted directly from: Canter, P. & Harries, K. (2004). Police officers' perceptions of maps and aerial photographs. Journal of Police Science and Management, *6(1), 37-50.*

With the increasing adoption of geographic information systems (GIS) by police departments and other law enforcement agencies around the world, the issue of how effectively maps and related media communicate information has become germane. Canter and Harries surveyed a small sample of police officers in order to test the utility of alternative visualizations of crime data presented at varying geographic scales. Their ultimate objective was to enhance understanding of the effectiveness of maps and aerial photographs commonly used in the context of various investigative, community, managerial, and other applications of GIS tools.

With due caution for the unrepresentative and small sample size that was used, their findings should at least be considered when designing maps for police personnel. The study highlights the importance of understanding your audience(s) and, thus, making finished maps that will effectively communicate findings. Even when presenting results from the same GIS analysis to different groups of people (i.e. policy-makers, police officers, academics), remember that you should (re)design and present your maps to each unique group as appropriate. The following are generalized findings:

1. The interpretation and use of large-scale crime maps can be improved when aerial photography and building footprints are introduced to the display. As a group, officers favored a combination map to view crime at the neighborhood scale.
2. Officers were able to relate the location of a crime incident to other map features such as buildings, wooded areas, and parking lots. Several officers commented on the utility of aerial photographs and building footprints to identify possible ingress/egress points or offender travel paths. Officers noted the location of auto theft locations within parking lots, which they were unable to do using centerline maps.
3. Officers generally believed that aerial photographs and building footprints improved their ability to read and interpret a crime map.
4. Centerline maps tended to be more useful when displayed at an intermediate or community scale. Unlike the neighborhood scale crime map, officers tended to dislike the introduction of building footprints to a community-scaled centerline map.
5. Aerial photographs improved the visualization of mapped crime data, particularly when displayed at a large scale. The utility of neighborhood centerline maps for showing the location of crime improved when building footprints and aerial photographs were added to the view.

DOWNLOADING CENSUS SHAPEFILES

1. Download a census geography (i.e. tract or block group) shapefile for one county at a time from any part of the country. You can do this from the Esri TIGER site:

   a. http://www.census.gov/geo/www/tiger/tgrshp2010/tgrshp2010.html

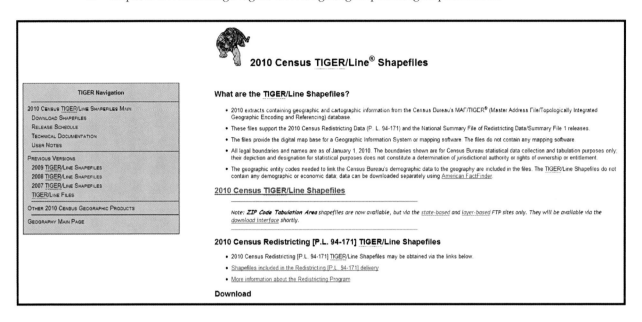

2. In ArcMap or ArcCatalog: Define that shapefile as geographic, e.g., NAD 1983 (because it is unprojected). Then, project that shapefile into the appropriate regional projection (e.g., state plane).

3. You can download SF1 (short-form) data from the Esri site for tracts, block groups, or blocks, but this only includes basic age, sex, race, household composition and own/rent data, so you will likely need to download SF3 (long-form) census data from the US Census Bureau site.

Diagram illustrating the legal and statistical entities for which the Census Bureau tabulates data during the decennial census. (Source: U.S. Census Bureau, Geography Division. Created: January 17, 2002.)

MAP PROJECTIONS

Projections manage the distortion that is inevitable when a (mostly) spherical earth is viewed as a flat map. All projection systems distort geography in some way— either by distorting area, shape, distance, direction, or scale. There are dozens of different projection systems in use since different systems work best in different parts of the Earth; even within the same parts of the Earth, GIS users have different priorities and needs. The tools for working with projections in ArcGIS are relatively advanced particularly in their ability to re-project layers with different projection systems "on the fly."

Recognizing the Coordinate System

 From ArcMap: Right-click the layer you wish to work with, click "**Properties…**" and select the "**Source**" tab. **Or, From ArcCatalog**: right-click the layer you wish to work with, click "**Properties…**" and select "**XY Coordinate System**".

Map layers can be drawn according to a geographic coordinate system or projected coordinate system. Geographic coordinate systems indicate location using longitude and latitude based on a sphere (or spheroid) while projected coordinate systems use X and Y based on a plane. As long as computer screens and printed maps are flat, projected coordinate systems will be more appropriate for working with GIS data. Often you will not know the coordinate system used, particularly if you inherit data or download it from the Internet. If you are lucky, the shapefile will include a .proj file which contains information about the coordinate system. If there is no projection information, you can map the data to determine its coordinate system. If the map units displayed in the gray bar below your map are in degrees, seconds, and minutes, then you know the data are in a

`75°12'21.37"W  40°0'37.82"N`

geographic coordinate system. You may also recognize this because your maps look distorted. Map layers in geographic coordinate systems are sometimes described as "unprojected." Map layers downloaded from the US Census Bureau are generally unprojected.

Projecting Unprojected Shapefiles

 From ArcMap: open "**ArcToolbox**" by clicking 🔴, click "**Data Management Tools**" and select "**Projections and Transformations**". Select the "**Define Projection**" tool. **Or, From ArcCatalog**: right-click the layer you wish to work with, click "**Properties…**" and select "**XY Coordinate System**". Click the "**Select…**" button.

⚠ *If you are projecting a raster image, use the "Project Raster" tool under "Raster" toolbox (also within the "Projections and Transformations" toolbox).*

In most cases you will want to convert unprojected map layers—those with a geographic coordinate system—to projected map layers. There are two steps involved in this process. First, you must create a .proj file "defining" the map layer as unprojected; then you can "project" the map layer using the projection of your choice.

In the "**Define Projection**" tool's dialog box, choose a dataset (e.g. shapefile) as the input. If you added the relevant map layer to ArcMap, you will be able to find it in the dropdown menu. Otherwise you will need to click on the "folder icon" button to locate your map layer. Then you can choose the coordinate system using the

button.

From the "Shapefile Properties" dialog box, click the "Select" button, then choose "Geographic Coordinate Systems," "North America," and "NAD 1983 Datum." Click the "Add" button, then click "OK" on the Spatial Reference Properties dialog, then "OK" on the "Define Projection" tool.

You should not notice a difference in how the map layer is drawn as a result of defining the coordinate system. As a result of defining it, there is now a .proj file associated with your map layer and you can look at the detailed spatial reference information. Before you define a layer as unprojected, ArcGIS will refer to it as "assumed geographic." In order to project the map layer, open the "Define Projection" tool again. Click on the

button to the right of "Output Coordinate System" to choose your projection. Click on the "Select" button on the "Spatial Reference Properties" dialog box, then choose "Projected Coordinate Systems." Now you need to choose your projection. For relatively small areas like Philadelphia, the differences in projection systems (the distortion in shape, area, distance, direction, and scale) are minimal. You are best choosing whatever projection system is most commonly used. In Philadelphia, that is State Plane 1983 (feet) Pennsylvania South. After making your selection, click "OK." ArcGIS may indicate that there is a "Datum conflict between map and output." In order to map your newly projected layer, create a new ArcMap document.

Working with Projected Map Layers

Sometimes the map layers you receive will already be projected but will not carry a .proj file so you do not know the projection. If you download the data, be sure to read any metadata files that may contain information about the project. If someone has sent you the map layers, ask them about the projection. If these approaches fail, try mapping the data. You may recognize that the data are projected by the units showing in the gray bar below the map. If they are not in longitude and latitude, they are probably projected. As you work with a particular projection system, you will come to recognize the map units and range of coordinate values. For example, State Plane coordinates for Philadelphia are generally in feet and look like 2691607.78, 246268.98. UTM coordinates will be in meters and look like 486850.72, 4430095.19.

When you add a shapefile to ArcMap that the software recognizes as being projected but has no .proj file, ArcMap will usually warn you that spatial reference information is missing. Data that are projected but missing spatial reference information will look fine when they are drawn, but you may not be able to use ArcMap's "on the fly" projection capabilities, measurement tools, spatial join, or geoprocessing functions.

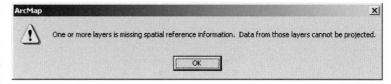

If you know the proper projection, you can use the "Define Projection" tool in ArcToolbox. You will need to select the projection from the "Projected Coordinate Systems." If a map layer is already projected AND defined, you can change the projection using the same tool. *NOTE: You must add the re-projected shapefile to a new ArcMap document to see the results.*

Troubleshooting with Projections

If you are unable to draw your map layers together or if your distance units do not make sense, you are likely experiencing a problem with projections. If you are not able to figure out the problem, you may want to show your shapefiles to someone with more GIS experience. It is easy to get confused while using the "Define Projection" and "Project" wizards, and frequently the more you try to fix the problem, the more mixed up your projections get. Stay calm and do not be ashamed to ask for help. You may also have luck returning to your original files.

 Make a copy of the original shapefiles before messing with the projection.

Defining Projection for a Data Frame

Ideally, you will specify the projection of each of your map layers. Alternatively, you can set the projection for your Data Frame for your map document. All of the map layers listed under the "Layers" icon in your table of contents are in the same data frame (you can have multiple data frames in the same map document).

From the Table of Contents: right-click the data frame you wish to work with, click "**Properties...**" and select the "**Coordinate System**" tab.

The Data Frame will automatically assume the Geographic or Projected Coordinate System of the first shapefile that is added to ArcMap. If subsequent shapefiles are unprojected, or in a different coordinate system than the data frame, ArcMap may notify you to this effect prior to (temporarily) re-projecting the shapefile on-the-fly.

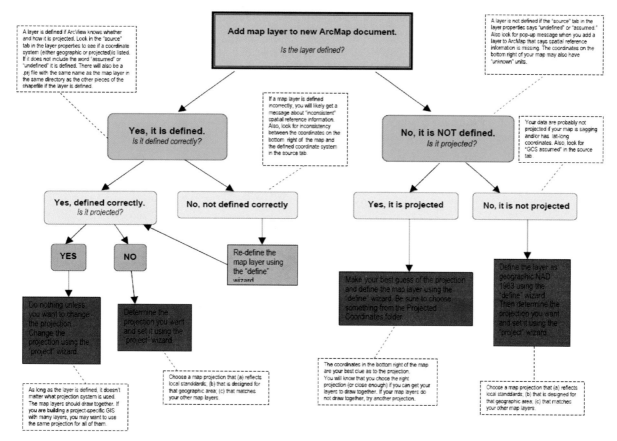

Diagram courtesy of: Amy Hillier, PhD

CREATING NEW SHAPEFILES FROM EXISTING SHAPEFILES

From the Table of Contents: right-click the layer you wish to work with, click "**Data**" and select "**Export Data...**".

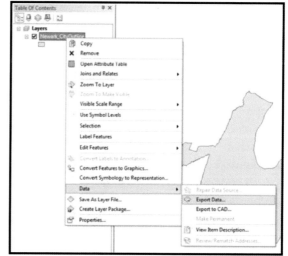

This makes a separate duplicate shapefile. In the "Export Data" dialog box, give your new file a name and location. The resulting shapefile will have the exact same features and variables in the attribute table as the original shapefile.

You can create a new shapefile that only includes your selected map features by right-clicking on its layer name in the Table of Contents → Data → Export Data. Choose the appropriate radio button regarding coordinate systems (you'll probably want the default). Make sure you have "**Selected features**" chosen in the "**Export**" drop down box. Select a location and name for the output shapefile and then click the "OK" button.

Data Frame projections are temporary, shapefile projections are (or should be) permanent. However, if you want to quickly and permanently project an unprojected shapefile that is within a Data Frame of the desired Projected Coordinate System, then the "Export Data" function is a good method. In the "Export Data" dialog box, under "Use the same coordinate system as:", select the radio button next to "the data frame." This will automatically create a new shapefile that will be permanently projected with the same coordinate system as the Data Frame.

USING EXCEL SPREADSHEET FILES

Add Excel files to ArcMap in the same manner you would add any other data, such as a shapefile (i.e. Click the "Add Data" button). The name of the Excel file that will appear in the Table of Contents in ArcMap is the name of the Worksheet (i.e. those 3 tabs at the bottom of the screen that read "Sheet1", "Sheet2", "Sheet3", and appear by default when you open a new Excel spreadsheet). Therefore, you should change the name of the Excel "Worksheet Tab" that you will import to something meaningful (When you add the Excel Spreadsheet file to ArcMap, it will prompt you to choose to one of the Worksheets). Since ArcGIS only permits 10 characters or less as attribute table column headings, you should change the column names in the Excel Worksheet to be 10 or fewer characters, with no spaces, to prevent undesired truncation.

CONVERTING FILES TO .DBF

Although ArcGIS imports Excel files directly from .XLS format, it still creates and exports attribute tables as DBF files. That is, DBF is still the primary and preferred format. So it is good to know how to convert files to DBF should the need ever arise. You can use Excel, SPSS, ACCESS, or other statistical and database packages. In many cases, Excel will be the only software available for the job.

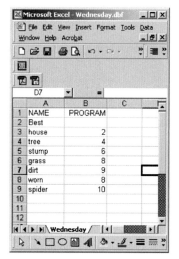

Excel can open a wide variety of formats, including delimited or fixed width text, Lotus, Quattro Pro, and web pages. If you are working with one of these other formats and need to make changes to your data in Excel, it is probably best to save the document as an Excel worksheet. When you save an Excel document, you can choose another format using the "Save As" options. But even if you choose .dbf at this stage, you may encounter problems. For example, your new .dbf file may not include all of the cells in your original file, or the columns may be formatted as strings rather than numbers.

Here are some things you can do to increase the odds of preserving your data during the conversion:

1. Limit your column headings to 10 characters. Excel will let you have infinitely long column names, but ArcMap will shrink them. It is better to come up with your own abbreviated names than to risk losing important information when ArcMap truncates the names.
2. Check your columns to be sure that they are formatted correctly as strings (left justified) or numbers (right justified). Also, look for rows at the very top that may be blank or contain data that are different from the following cells. For example, you may have a column named "programs" with values ranging from 2-10 for all of your cells, but the first cell is blank or has an "NR" for "not reported." This column will be formatted as a string when you convert to .dbf and open it in ArcMap—because .dbf takes its cue from the first data cell in the column. To avoid this problem, you can sort the data so that the blank cell is not on top, or you can put in an appropriate numeric value (such as 0 or 999 for missing data). You can convert a string field to numeric in ArcMap, but it is easier if you start with the right format.
3. When you are ready to save your data, highlight all of the cells that contain values (including the column names). From the Insert menu, go to "Name" and "Define." Type in a name (type anything; it doesn't matter), click "Add" and "OK." This increases the likelihood that all of your cells will be included in the new table. Now you can save your document. First, save all changes in your Excel document. Then, from the File menu, choose "Save As" and select "DBF4" from the dropdown menu. First Excel will give you a warning that the .dbf format doesn't support multiple worksheets and that only the data in the top (active) worksheet will be saved. Click "OK." Excel will then give you a second warning message because .dbf is very different from .xls and some formatting may be lost. Just click "OK."

If you do not get BOTH of these warnings, then the conversion to DBF was not successful. Try it again by copying everything into a new workbook.

When you close Excel, Excel will prompt you again with these messages, as though it is still incredulous that you would choose any format other than Microsoft's. Humor the software and go through these two steps again. As soon as you add your table to ArcMap, look it over to make sure that all of the data came through and are in the right format.

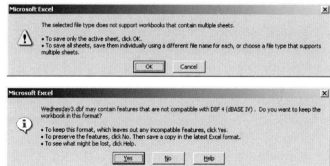

Before converting an Excel spreadsheet to DBF...

	Your table must have a column with Unique ID numbers for each row	All data must be fully visible. If necessary, ← Expand column widths→			
Your table must have a row with column headings/names	ID	Address	Crime_Type	Crime_Date	Conviction
	1	123 Main St	Robbery	1/25/99	Y
	2	30th St & Walnut St	Theft	1/26/99	Y
	3	1776 University Ave	Burglary	1/01/99	N
	...	...	...	...	...
	1000	900 Cooper Pl	Car Jacking	1/15/99	Y

- Highlight all of the data in your table before "Saving As" a DBF 4 (dBASE IV). Only data that is highlighted and visible in each field will be converted.

- There's NO NEED to use **bold** or *italic* formats—these formats will not transfer to the DBF file. "Center," "Left" and "Right" formatting alignments will not transfer either.

- When Saving As a DBF, you will receive multiple warnings from Excel that the DBF version may mess up the formatting. Just say "yes" and "OK." Close Excel before adding the new DBF file to ArcMap.

- It is recommended to save your table as both an Excel (.xls) file and a dBASE (.dbf) file. That way, you can always go back to the original Excel file to make changes if necessary.

GIS DATA FORMAT AND DATA CLEANING

GIS mapping follows the time tested theorem "garbage in, garbage out". If your addresses are not clean, then you are significantly increasing the probability that they will not be geocoded correctly. Cleaning addresses means:

- Retaining only the key address elements in one field: house/building number; street name; street type (e.g., 100 Main St)
- Getting rid of all extraneous characters (e.g., "BSMT" "REAR" "APT 1" "UNIT 3", etc.)
- Standardizing spelling (e.g., converting all incidences of "Mass Ave" to "Massachusetts Ave")
- Removing all irrelevant punctuation including commas, quotation marks, apostrophes, parentheses, dashes, etc. that may interfere with the application's coding and can cause an error. Periods are not needed after abbreviations, such as street types.
- Changing street address ranges (e.g. "110-114 Main St") to only one number (e.g. "110 Main St")
- Finding appropriate street addresses for building or location names (e.g. "Wynnwood Apartments", "Homeless Shelter")
- Standardizing cross streets (e.g. use ampersand [&])

Some examples:

Record #	Original Address	"Cleaned"
1	677 Huntington, #304	677 Huntington
2	46 Burr REAR	46 Burr St
3	Unit B, 1200 Comm Ave.	1200 Commonwealth Ave
4	423 Allston St., 4th Floor, Suite 100	423 Allston St
5	The Landmark Building, 401 Park Drive	401 Park Drive
6	99 ½ Chauncey St	99 Chauncey St
7	111-113 Walnut Street	111 Walnut Street
8	Main St and Chestnut Ave	Main St & Chestnut Ave

Address information should comprise 4 fields: Street Address, City, State, and ZIP code (last 4 digits of a ZIP should be in a separate field).

"Correct"

Record	Address	City	State	ZIP
1	677 Huntington Ave	Boston	MA	02115

"Incorrect"

Record	Address
1	677 Huntington Ave, Boston, MA 02115

X-Y coordinates should comprise two separate fields. Do not round the numbers.

For example:

Record	X	Y	Provider
1	2672973.889167	222351.750051	Safe Meadows Healthcare Center

Another example:

Record	X	Y	Provider
1	-75.238221	39.916205	Safe Meadows Healthcare Center

GIS-FRIENDLY DATASETS

- Must have spatial location: i.e. Street address, ZIP code, State, Tract, XY
- Must have a unique ID number
- Can include any other variables about each observation. Different variables should be in separate columns.
- Column/heading names must be 10 or fewer characters; No spaces.

ID	Location	Variable1	Variable2	Variable3
0001	123 Main St	Medical	Male	Refusal
0002	33rd St & Park Pl	Trauma	Female	Transport
0003	227 Penn Ave	Trauma	Male	Transport

Data is taken literally in a GIS. Differences in spacing, case, or coding can cause problems. Each field in the example to the right is different as far as GIS software is concerned, even though they all refer to the City of Newark.

Newark
NEWARK
Nwk
newark
City of Newark
Brick City

GIS programs differentiate data by the type of information entered into the database. Data can be numerical (i.e., 19104) or string (i.e. Pennsylvania). The ZIP code 19104 entered as *numerical* is <u>not the same</u> as 19104 entered as a *string*. Consider in advance the format your data should take. This might be dependent on the type of analyses or outputs you want to produce. Numbers, for example, can be added or subtracted while text strings cannot.

CHAPTER FIVE

Geocoding Addresses and Working with XY Coordinates

GEOCODING

Geocoding refers to the process of transforming street addresses into map features. In order to geocode, you need to have a table with addresses and a shapefile for streets that matches the geographic extent of your addresses. Through the geocoding process, ArcGIS will create a new point shapefile by matching each street name and number in your table to a place along a line segment in your street shapefile that represents a certain range of house numbers.

Preparing Tabular Data

In order to geocode, you need a table (.xls, .dbf or comma-delimited text) that has a field with street addresses. If the parts of the address—house number, street direction, street name, and designation/type—are in separate fields, you will need to collapse these into a single field. Having a separate field with the ZIP code can also be helpful.

Creating an Address Locator

  From ArcCatalog: right-click the folder you wish to store the Address Locator, click "**New**" and select "**Address Locator...**".

Several things should be considered when choosing an address locator style, including the type of geometry in your reference data and the format of address data you wish to search. For example, "US Streets with Zone" is a common locator style. First, it zeros in on a specific ZIP code area, and then finds an address on a specific side of a street within that ZIP. This is useful when your study area encompasses multiple jurisdictions that have the same street names. For example, if my study area is Essex County, NJ, "Main Street" might be the same name of different roads in the neighboring cities of Newark and Irvington. "US Streets with Zone" would ensure that the geocoded point is placed at the address in the correct city (i.e. the address in the correct ZIP code area).

From the chosen Address Locator (i.e. US Streets with Zone) window, you need to define the properties associated with the specific Address Locator. Reference Data is a shapefile that includes information about all of the streets in your area. A street centerline shapefile is made up of line segments that represent certain ranges of house numbers. The line segments also contain information in their attribute table about which side has even and odd house numbers. Where it says "**Reference Data**", click the button with the "Folder icon" to browse to your street shapefile and click the "Add" button. In the "**Field Map**" section, ArcGIS may be able to identify the appropriate fields on its own. If no field names appear in the drop down menus, or if they do not look right to you, you'll need to identify them yourself. The "**Input Address Fields**" section allows you to identify the names for the field(s) in your tabular data that contain the street address information. The "**Matching Options**" section allows you to indicate the level of sensitivity for the matching process. Essentially, ArcGIS needs to match the house numbers and street names in your tabular data with information in the street shapefile's attribute table (reference data). If the spelling of the street name is slightly different or an appropriate range of house numbers cannot be located, ArcGIS will assign the match a less than perfect score (100 is a perfect match). ArcGIS can geocode based on street intersections in addition to specific house numbers. In the "**Intersections**" section you can identify symbols (or "AND") used in your tabular data to indicate intersections. The "**Side Offset**" option allows you to place points slightly away from the middle of the street centerline file. While ArcView will know what side of the street your address falls on, your points will appear to fall directly on the centerline unless you specify an offset (i.e. 15-20 feet is usually adequate). If you check "**X and Y coordinates**" under the "**Output Fields**" section, ArcGIS will add X and Y fields to the new (geocoded) point shapefile's attribute table. Once you click "OK," a new address locator will be created. Once you create an address locator, you do not need to do it again (unless you go to a new computer).

Geocoding Addresses

 From the Standard toolbar on ArcMap: click on "**Customize**", select "**Toolbars**" and activate the "**Geocoding**" toolbar. Once activated, click the "**Geocode Addresses**" icon.

 You do not need to have your street layer (reference data) added to your map document to geocode data.

In the "**Choose an Address Locator to use…**" window, select the appropriate Address Locator or, if necessary, click the "**Add**" button and navigate to the folder where the "Address Locator" is located. After finding your address locator, click "Add," then click "OK."

On the next screen ("Geocode Addresses:" dialog window), you need to select the tabular file with the addresses you want to geocode. Then select the field in the table that contains the street address; choose a name and location for the new point shapefile that will be created (output). The "Geocoding Options" button gives you access to many of the same options available when you create an address locator. When you click "OK," ArcMap begins the geocoding process. The next screen indicates how well ArcMap was able to match the addresses. When you click the "Close" button, a new point shapefile should appear in the Table of Contents.

If you open the attribute table associated with the shapefile, you will see that the geocoding process added several fields to your original address table. The "Status" field indicates whether the record was matched (M) or left unmatched (U). The "Score" field indicates how closely the record matched the street centerline file. The "Side" field indicates on which side of the street the address was matched. The "Arc_Street" field is the address used in the match. This will be the same as the original address unless you edit it during the "Interactive Review."

Interactive Review and Rematching Addresses

 Click the "**Rematch**" button from the "**Geocoding Addresses…**" results window.

You will need to start an edit session in order to proceed with the "**Interactive Rematch**" process. The interactive review process can be used to correct and then match the unmatched or poorly matched records. For smaller data sets, it is especially important to review the unmatched records.

From the "Interactive Rematch" dialog box, you can edit the addresses in order to get a match/better match (do not worry, this only changes the address that ArcMap uses for geocoding; it does not change the data in your original table of addresses). Before you begin reviewing addresses, click the "**Show results**" drop-down menu to display only the addresses you are interested in reviewing. For instance, rather than scrolling through all the Matched or Tied addresses, you might only be interested in reviewing the "Unmatched" addresses. In addition, you also have the ability to pick a particular candidate and zoom to its location by clicking the "**Zoom to Candidates**" button. If you are familiar with the area, you may be able to visually access the accuracy of the candidate as well.

 To edit, search and match an address, within the "**Address**" section, click on the category of the address you wish to change (i.e. "City"). Make the appropriate changes and then click the "**Search**" button. ArcMap will list possible matches (along with their matching scores). Highlight the best candidate and click the "**Match**" button.

Street intersections are the most likely to create ties in the matching process. For example, ArcMap might not know whether to place the "10th and Market" point on 10th Street or just north or just south of Market Street. Most likely, it will not matter for your work. If it does, you are better off using a house number and street, rather than an intersection. Choosing the "Match If Candidates Tie" box in the geocoding options will help you avoid having to match these individually.

Determining an Acceptable Match Rate

A minimum reliable geocoding match rate is 85 percent[15]. Be sure to write down the match rate so that you can report it later. Often you will receive a list of addresses that contains some PO Box numbers or missing data that will prevent you from matching all your records. Other times your addresses will look fine but simply will not match the street centerline file. The most important thing to determine is if the error (the unmatched records) is random or systematic. If you have done all that you can to gather complete and accurate addresses, random error is acceptable and probably unavoidable. Systematic error is not. Be sure to check for patterns in your unmatched records (either by interactively reviewing unmatched records or, after finishing geocoding, open the attribute table and sort by "status" to review all of the "U" (unmatched) records. There is no guarantee that the matched records will be mapped in the right place. Do a spot check with the "Identify" tool to make sure that records mapped somewhere that makes sense to you.

LOCATING AN INDIVIDUAL ADDRESS

If you only have one or two addresses to map, you can take a shortcut from the entire geocoding process. ArcMap provides two options to locate individual addresses.

From the Tools toolbar: click , activate the "**Locations**" tab and select a locator from the "**Choose a locator**" dropdown. Key in the address in the "**Single Line Input**" and click "**Find**". It may be useful to check the "**Show all candidates**" option (this will display all potential matches, even those that fall below your accuracy threshold).

Or, From the "Geocoding" toolbar: select an address locator from the dropdown menu, type in the address in the "**Single Line Input**" space and hit "Enter" on your keyboard.

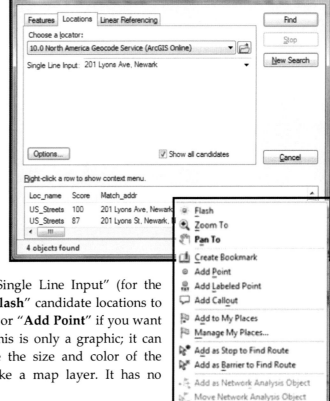

Once the address location is found, you have several mapping options. Just right-click one of the addresses (for the first option, above) or right-click the address you entered in the "Single Line Input" (for the second option, above). You might choose to "**Flash**" candidate locations to make sure ArcGIS is mapping in the right area or "**Add Point**" if you want a marker at the location. Keep in mind that this is only a graphic; it can easily be deleted or moved. You can change the size and color of the graphic, but you cannot turn it on or off like a map layer. It has no attributes associated with it.

CREATING XY COORDINATES FROM ADDRESSES

You can instruct the geocoding process to create XY coordinates for each point—this is one of the options when you create the Address Locator. **Or, from the "Geocode Addresses" window**: select the "**Geocoding Options...**" button and check the "**X and Y coordinates**" option within the "**Output Fields**" section.

Output Fields	
☑ X and Y coordinates	☐ Standardized address
☐ Reference data ID	☐ Percent along

DISPLAYING XY DATA

Sometimes you will need to map a table that only has X and Y coordinates identifying specific locations but no shapefile associated with it. This might occur because a GPS (global positioning system) unit was used to collect the data or because that is the way a private vendor has chosen to distribute the data. A table with X and Y coordinates is much easier to distribute than a shapefile, because it is smaller, does not involve multiple files, and is not ArcGIS-specific. In order to map the data in ArcGIS, the X and Y values will need to be included as separate columns in an Excel, dBASE or delimited text file. You can add the table to ArcMap just as you would a shapefile (with the "Add Data" button), but you do not need to add it to ArcMap in order to map it.

From the Standard toolbar: click "**Geoprocessing**"and select "**ArcToolbox**", or click [icon] on the Tools toolbar. Click "**Data Management Tools**", select "**Features**" and click "**Add XY Coordinates**".

From the "**Add XY Coordinates**" dialog box, browse to the table with the XY data. Since ArcMap will find the appropriate fields in your table, it is important to have the table you are using be "prepped" and "cleaned" (i.e. separate columns for X and Y coordinates). As with shapefiles, tables with XY data that you acquire may be projected. If the Spatial Reference "**Description**" box reads "**Unknown Coordinate System**", then they are unprojected.

Add the XY table by clicking [icon] . **Or, From the Table of Contents**: right-click the table you wish to work with and select "**Display XY Data...**". Specify the appropriate fields and "**Edit...**" coordinate system, if necessary.

ADDING XY COORDINATES (CENTROIDS) TO POINTS, LINES OR POLYGONS

Just as you may need to convert a table with XY data into a map layer, you may need to add XY coordinates to an existing layer containing points, lines or polygons. Before you are able to add XY coordinates, you may need to add new columns to your shapefile's attribute table.

From the Table of Contents: right-click the layer you wish to work with and click "**Open Attribute Table**". Click ▦ ▾ and select "**Add Field…**". Create both X and Y columns with the "**Type**" for both being "Double".

Once you have created your new columns, you can calculate the geometry of your coordinates.

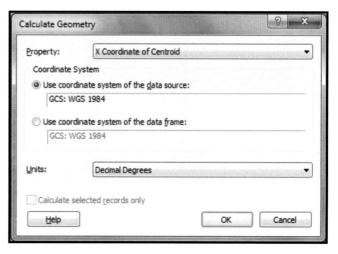

Right-click the top of your new column (i.e. X) and select "**Calculate Geometry…**". A message might appear warning that you are about to calculate outside of an edit session. Acknowledge this by clicking the "OK" button. In the "**Calculate Geometry**" window, select the new property from the "**Property**" dropdown box (i.e. X Coordinate of Centroid). Click "OK" and ArcMap will calculate the X-coordinate for each point in the shapefile. Repeat for the Y-coordinates.

You can check the new XY-coordinates that were created in the attribute table by mapping them.

Right-click the newly exported table and select "**Display XY Data…**". Specify the appropriate fields and "**Edit…**" coordinate system, if necessary.

CHAPTER SIX

Spatial and Tabular Joins

JOINING TABLES

Tabular joins use a common unique identifier to attach an attribute table to a shapefile. Often you will have attributes stored in a separate table that you want to join to a shapefile in order to display that data. This is especially common with census data, when you will often obtain census attribute data (SF1 or SF3) in files separate from the shapefiles for census tracts, blockgroups or other units of analysis. Tables to be joined with shapefiles must be in either the DBF or Excel file format.

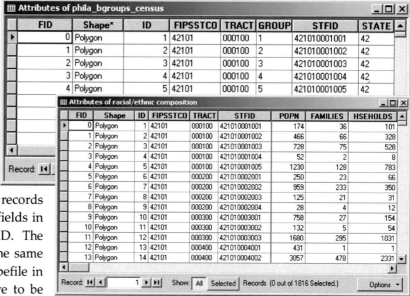

From the Table of Contents: right-click the layer you wish to work with, select "**Joins and Relates**" and click "**Join…**".

Identifying a Key (Step 1)

In order to join an attribute table to a shapefile, you must identify a field that is common to your attribute table and the attribute table associated with your shapefile. This field is known as a key, or unique identifier, because it uniquely identifies each record in your table and shapefile on which ArcGIS can join, or match, your data. The values must be formatted in an identical way (i.e. numerical, string). If they are not, you must edit one of the fields or create a new field and recalculate the values so that their formats match perfectly.

The attribute table (right) of a census tract shapefile contains multiple fields that uniquely identify each record (e.g. STFID). The other table (to the right) includes several attributes of census tracts but cannot be mapped until it is joined to a shapefile. There is one field that uniquely identifies records and, thus, can be used to match fields in the census tract shapefile: STFID. The field name does not have to be the same in the attribute table and the shapefile in order to join them; they just have to be formatted in the same way.

While you may most often perform joins on census data, you can also join attributes to shapefiles for other data: e.g., zipcodes, school districts, counties. You can join on a name (such as neighborhood name, or the name of an institution), although keep in mind that differences in spelling and spacing will prevent records from joining.

Joining a Table (Step 2)

Keep in mind that ArcMap does not check to make sure that the key fields or their formats match, so you should double-check them (by opening both tables) before performing the join.

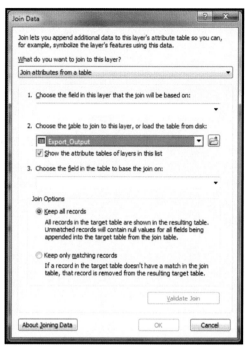

 From the "Join Data" window: select "Join attributes from a table" from the "What do you want to join with this layer?" dropdown menu. In the dropdown menu under "Choose the field in this layer that the join will be based on" (item 1), select the key field in your shapefile. In the dropdown menu under "Choose the table to join to this layer, or load the table from disk" (item 2), select the table you wish to join to the shapefile (the table does not need to be added to ArcMap first). In the dropdown menu under "Choose the field in the table to base the join on" (item 3), select the key field in your table (from item 2) that you wish to join.

Under the "Join Options" section, indicate what you want ArcMap to do if all of the map features in the shapefile do not have a match in the attribute table, or vice versa. The default is to "Keep all records", meaning that some map features might have no values for some fields. Individual records might not match because of problems with the key or because there are different numbers of records in each of your files. When you open your shapefile's attribute table after a successful join, there should be new fields that contain the data from your table. The new field names will include the name of the attribute table from which it came.

When you perform an attribute join the data is dynamically joined together. This means that nothing is written to disk and the join holding the data together is not permanent.

 To make the join permanent, right-click on the shapefile layer in the Table of Contents, click "Data" and select "Export Data…". This works like a "Save as," so it creates a new shapefile. The resulting shapefile will have variable names that are much shorter than those in the table created during the temporary join, and it will include attributes from both (or all) joined tables.

⚠ *Several tables or layers can be joined to a single table or layer; relationship class joins can be mixed with attribute joins.*

REMOVING JOINS

 From the Table of Contents: right-click the layer you wish to work with, select "Joins and Relates" and click "Remove Join(s)". You have the option of removing a specific join or all joins.

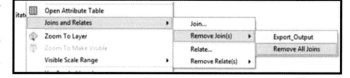

When a join is removed, all data from tables that were joined after it are also removed, but data from previously joined tables remain. Symbology or labeling that is based on an appended column is returned to a default state when the join is removed. *NOTE: Spatial joins create a new shapefile, so there is nothing to "remove"; delete the new shapefile if you do not want the result of a spatial join.*

SPATIAL JOINS

Spatial joins use common geography to append fields from one layer, or information about a layer, to another layer. This allows you to assign the characteristics of an area—such as a census tract or school district—to individual houses, individuals, or events as well as to aggregate points by areas.

 From the Table of Contents: right-click the layer you wish to work with, select "**Joins and Relates**" and click "**Joins…**".

Assigning Area Characteristics to Points

Using a spatial join, you can identify which area a point falls within. For example, you might need to determine in what census tract each of your study participants live. You must have a point layer and a polygon layer in ArcMap in order to do this.

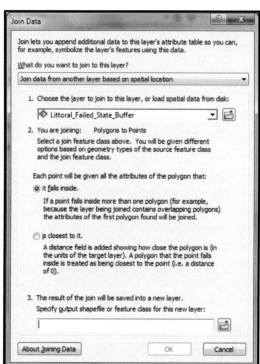

 In the first dropdown menu of the "Join Data" dialog box, indicate that you want to "**Join data to that layer based on spatial location**". In the next dropdown menu, choose your polygon layer. Next, choose the first radio button so that Each point is given all the attributes of the polygon "**it falls inside**". If you have points outside your polygon (for example, if you have a census tract map of Philadelphia with points representing addresses in the city and just outside it), choose the second radio button. Specify the name and location of the new point shapefile.

The resulting point shapefile will have many new columns as your polygon shapefile. This may include only the polygon identifier (such as the census tract number) or the identifier and attributes.

Aggregating Points to Lines or Polygons

Using a spatial join, you can determine how many points fall in each polygon feature. For example, you might need to determine how many crimes occurred within each police district. You must have a point layer and a polygon layer in ArcMap in order to do this.

In the first dropdown menu of the "Join Data" dialog box, indicate that you want to "**Join data to that layer based on spatial location**". In the next dropdown menu, choose your point layer. Next, the radio button should be set for "**Each polygon will be given a summary of the numeric attributes of the points that fall inside it, and a count field showing how many points fall inside it.**" If your points do not all fall within your polygons (for example, you have a map of city council districts and points representing addresses in the city and just outside it), choose the second radio button, instead. You can then decide if you want to summarize the attributes of your points by their areas in the boxes below. Finally, specify the name and location of the new area shapefile.

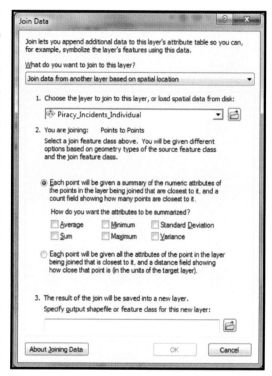

If you did not check any of the boxes to summarize the attributes of the points, your new shapefile will have only one new field named "Count_". This will indicate how many points fall into each polygon. You will probably want to change the name to something that you will remember (by creating a new field called "TheftCount," for example, and calculating it as equal to "Count_"). Now you can use this count value as the basis of a thematic map.

DOWNLOADING AND JOINING CENSUS ATTRIBUTE DATA

1. Go to the US Census Bureau website www.census.gov. Follow the link for American Factfinder and then data sets (buttons on left). Note that as of February 2011, the new American Factfinder became available (http://factfinder2.census.gov/faces/nav/jsf/pages/index.xhtml).
2. Select your data set. SF3 is the census long form, so it contains the most data.
3. Select either "detailed tables" or "custom tables" (if you want to pick individual variables from within census tables… this is more involved but gives you greater flexibility).
4. Choose your geography. If you want census tracts, select that from the first dropdown menu, then choose your state and county. Be sure to choose "All Census Tracts." If you want block groups, first choose the "Geo Within Geo" tab at the top of the page, then choose block groups from the first drop-down menu. If you want all the block groups within the county (most likely), choose "county," then your state and county. Be sure to choose "All Block Groups" at the end. Click "add" then "next." Be sure to let the website refresh fully after each step before you make your next selection.

5. Choose your variables. You may find it easiest to use the "By Subject" or "By Keyword" tabs so you can see the variables listed by topics of interest to you. If you used the "custom table" option, put a check mark next to the box for each variable you want (see below); only these will be downloaded. Be sure to include an appropriate denominator (it will usually be listed first, as "total" as in total people who answered this question). If you used the "detailed tables" option, you will download all of the variables within a particular table which will include a denominator.

6. Go the "Print/Download" option from the blue header to download your data. Save as an Excel table. This will automatically transpose the records, so each row will represent a geographic unit (such as a census tract) and each column will represent a different variable.

7. Unzip your files. You will only need the Excel file that ends with the word "data."

8. Open the Excel table. Change the column names to be 10 or fewer characters, with no spaces in the names, so you can bring this into ArcMap. Create a data dictionary, if necessary, to remember what each variable means. Be sure to have only one row with column names (when you open the table, there will be two). Confirm that one of the geographic identifiers matches the geographic identifiers in your corresponding shapefile. Save your file with these changes.

9. Add your table to ArcMap. Look at it and make sure the columns imported correctly.

10. Join the table to an appropriate shapefile. Check to make sure your join worked. Make a permanent copy of the joined table and shapefile. Right click on the shapefile, go to data and export, then save a new copy. Yes, do add it to the map when you are done.

⚠️ *You may need to calculate new values in your table in order to get the variable you want. If you use poverty, for example, you'll need to add three columns (income 50% or less than poverty line, 50-74%, and 75-99%) together to get the total number of people living below the poverty line.*

CHAPTER SEVEN

Working with Attribute Tables

ATTRIBUTE TABLES FOR SHAPEFILES

Every shapefile has an attribute table associated with it. The table will have as many rows, or records, as it does map features. The total number of records will be shown at the bottom of your table. There can be any number of columns, or fields.

Two are standard: FID (the feature ID) and Shape (which can be point, polyline, or polygon). The rest of the fields will vary. There should be a field that identifies each map feature with a unique name or number, such as a census tract number or neighborhood name. There may be additional fields identifying attributes of the map feature (type of crime at a particular address, number of people living in a census tract).

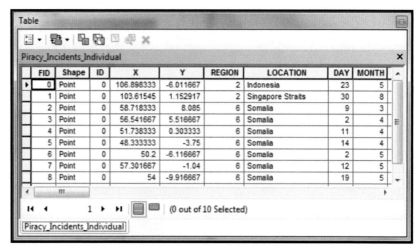

 From the Table of Contents: right-click layer you wish to work with and select "**Open Attribute Table**"

Within the "**Table**" window, you have a couple of tools and options readily accessible. Most of these tools and options are discussed in other sections of this
manual. The name of the tool or option can provide you with an idea of what it is supposed to do; thus, simply move the cursor over the tool or option to bring up the title.

OTHER TABLES

Often you will have data in a table separate from your shapefile. For example, you may have a census tract shapefile with no attribute information and a table with all of the 2010 census tract data. ArcGIS can read Excel (.xls), dBase (.dbf) and comma-delimited text tables, but will allow editing for only .dbf or .xls tables (you can convert .txt tables to .dbf in EXCEL, SPSS, ACCESS, or in ArcMap). You can add attribute tables to ArcMap just as you do shapefiles, using the "Add Data" button or, from the "File" menu, "Add Data." When you add a table, ArcMap will switch the table of contents from the "display" to the "source" tab. You can only see tables listed in the TOC when the "Source" tab is active. Open the table by right clicking on its name in the Table of Contents and click "Open."

You can work with tables—sort values, freeze columns, generate summary statistics, select records, and export tables—without worrying about corrupting your data. You cannot change any of the data in your table unless you go to "Start Editing" from the "Editor" toolbar. One exception is when adding new fields or deleting existing fields, both of which do not require you to start editing.

SORTING RECORDS

From the shapefile's attribute table: right-click the column name you wish to sort and select "**Sort Ascending**"/"**Sort Descending**".

You are also able to do multiple levels of sorting in a stepwise manner. For example, you can go from a greater level of spatial aggregation (i.e. global region) to a smaller level (i.e. specific location), while further sorting by month and day. Such multi-level sorting can be beneficial if you are attempting to visually assess certain relationships among data.

From the shapefile's attribute table: right-click the column name you wish to sort and select "**Advanced Sorting…**". A window will appear that provides up to four levels in which you are able to sort your data.

FREEZING COLUMNS

Freezing a column means that it will remain in view even as you scroll. This is particularly helpful if you wish to make changes to data but need to refer to the column name.

From the shapefile's attribute "**Table**", right-click the column name you wish to freeze and select "**Freeze/Unfreeze Column**". If you wish to unfreeze the column, simply follow the same procedure.

SUMMARY STATISTICS

You can view summary statistics for any numeric field (numeric fields are justified right). You can obtain summary statistics on additional fields from the "Field" drop down menu of the "Statistics" dialog box.

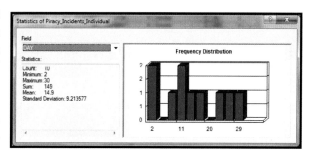

From the shapefile's attribute table: right-click column name you wish to obtain the statistics for and select "**Statistics…**".

SELECTING RECORDS

You can select a subset of your records to look at more closely.

 You can highlight an individual record (row) by clicking in the gray area at the far left side of the table. To highlight multiple records, hold the control key down. At the bottom of the table, ArcMap will indicate how many of the total records are highlighted. Click the "Show selected records" tool (see left) to view only the selected records. You can also switch selections using the "**Switch Selection**" tool and clear selections using the "**Clear Selection**" on the "Table" toolbar.

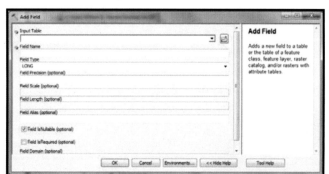

EXPORTING TABLES

 From the shapefile's attribute table: click 🔳 ▾ and select "**Export**".

ADD NEW COLUMN/FIELD

 From the shapefile's attribute table: click 🔳 ▾ and select "**Add Field...**". Or, From ArcToolbox: click "Data Management Tools", select "**Fields**" and click "**Add Field**"

⚠ *You may have difficulty adding a new field if you do not have permission to edit the table. Most likely, this is because the "read only" box is checked in the table properties. This happens automatically when you copy data from a CD. To change this, find your table on your hard drive (through Windows Explorer or My Computer, not through ArcCatalog), right click, and go to "properties." Remove the check mark next to "read only."*

From the "Add Field" dialog box, give your new field a name. Do not use ?,&,$,#,@,*,!,~ or spaces and keep your field name to 10 or fewer characters. From the dropdown menu choose the type of field. *Short Integer*: numeric, no decimal place, up to 19 characters. *Long Integer*: numeric, no decimal place, up to 19 characters. *Float*: numeric, with decimal place, (default is one place before decimal and 11 after). *Double*: numeric, with decimal place (default is 7 places before the decimal and 11 after). *Text*: numbers or letters, specify length (default = 50 characters). *Date*: can include time and date. *Blob*: up to four characters. Finally, determine the scale (number of places) and precision (number of places to the right of the decimal point), or accept the defaults by leaving them 0.

DELETE COLUMN/FIELD

 From the shapefile's attribute table: right-click the column name you wish to delete and select "Delete Field". **Or, From ArcToolbox**: click "**Data Management Tools**", select "**Fields**" and click "Delete Field"

Deleting a column/field using "Data Management Tools" may be useful when you want to delete multiple columns. You can even delete all the columns/fields of a shapefile if you wish!

 Delete columns/fields with caution! Changes will be permanent not just within your map document, but in your original file on your hard drive, as well.

CALCULATING VALUES OUTSIDE AN EDIT SESSION

In ArcMap you can edit values in an existing field or create a new field and calculate new values. Keep in mind that you cannot change the format (i.e. text, integer, long integer) of an existing column, so if you need to transform the format of a column, you will need to create a new field and copy data to it from an existing field.

 From the shapefile's attribute table: right-click the column name you wish to work with and select "**Field Calculator…**"

ArcMap will open the "Field Calculator" dialog box. If your value is a constant, you can simply type the value in the box at the bottom. More likely, your new value will be based on values in other fields, so you will need to use the calculator. You can create an expression by double clicking on the field names. For example, to calculate the percent of the population 65 and up, click on the field name with the total 65 and up, click on the "/" button, and click on the field name with the total population. If you edit a table outside an edit session, it is best to create new fields rather than to edit values in an existing field—since you cannot undo your work. With new fields, you can just delete a field and start over if you mess up.

 If any of the records in your table are highlighted, ArcMap will only perform calculations on the highlighted records.

Common Error when Calculating Values

ArcGIS will not allow you to divide by zero, so if the denominator (e.g. total population in the example above) is zero for any of your records, ArcGIS will not calculate any of the

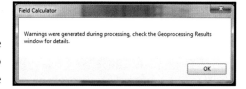

values and will display an error message. To get around this, you need to select only the records where the denominator is something other than zero.

Start by selecting the records with a zero in the denominator (because there are fewer of these). Do this by right-clicking the field with your denominator and sort ascending. Holding down the control key, highlight all the records that have a value of zero. From the "**Table Options**" button menu, choose "**Switch Selection**" or click so that all of the records with non-zero values are highlighted. Now you should be able to proceed with calculating values.

LOCATION QUOTIENTS

The location quotient is most frequently used in economic geography and locational analysis, but it has much wider applicability. The location quotient (LQ) is an index for comparing an area's share of a particular activity with the area's share of some basic or aggregate phenomenon. In other words, the LQ is a measure of the relative significance of a phenomenon (e.g. burglaries) in a region (Newark) compared with its significance in a larger ("benchmark") region (New Jersey). Or, put another way, LQ is a measure used to identify concentration within an area and is expressed as a ratio of the proportional share of the subjects at the local level (census tract) to the ratio of the total area covered (Philadelphia). Location quotients are calculated within the Attribute Table of a polygon feature class. Location quotient is expressed as: $LQ = (x_i/t_i) \, / \, (X/T)$

The numerator of equation is the percentage of the activity in area i, and the denominator is the percentage of the base. A location quotient is thus the ratio of two percentages and is therefore dimensionless. So, for example, referring to the equation above: xi might represent the number of persons in group x (e.g., study group) in census tract i; ti represents the total population of persons (e.g., general or poverty) in the particular census tract i; and X and T represent the city-wide number of persons in group x and population t, respectively. *NOTE: A common error occurs in ArcGIS when a calculation requires dividing by zero (0) for at least one record in the attribute table. Check your data and calculate again using only the "selected" records whose denominator will not be an attribute with the value of zero.*

If LQ>1 this indicates a relative concentration of the activity in area I, compared to the region as a whole.
If LQ =1the area has a share of the activity in accordance with its share of the base.
If LQ<1 the area has less of a share of the activity than is more generally, or regionally, found.

The formula for Location Quotients requires that something of interest (e.g., Index Crimes per County) be divided by some other meaningful variable, such as "square miles", "population", "number of sworn police officers", etc. Location Quotients are interpreted as "the likelihood of finding 'something' of interest in an area, given the other attribute about that area." In effect, the Location Quotient formula controls for the denominator variable. So, a question might be: "What is the likelihood of index crimes occurring in each county, given the number of people (i.e. population) who could commit a crime in that county?" Results less than 1 are not very likely, and the likelihood increases as values increase above 1.

Location quotient values, once calculated, can be displayed as a choropleth map.

ZOOM IN: Location Quotient Choropleth Maps[16]

Metraux, Caplan, Klugman and Hadley (2007) used location quotients (LQ) to assess the extent of residential segregation among 15,246 people diagnosed with severe mental illness (SMI) and receiving Medicaid (MA) in Philadelphia. Once location quotients were calculated in the Attributes Table of the Census Tract Shapefile, corresponding choropleth maps were constructed using Arcview. The figure below (left) shows areas of Philadelphia with elevated LQs for the study group based on using the general population of adults as the denominator for both local and overall proportions.

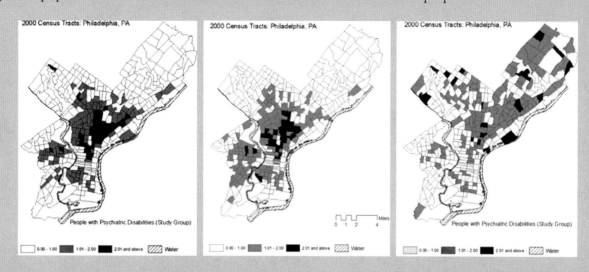

Location quotient values for adults (ages 18--64) living in households with incomes below the poverty threshold, based on their proportional representation among the overall adult population are presented in the figure above (middle). Census tracts with the highest LQs for the study group contained disproportionate shares of poor adults, which suggested that poverty should be controlled for. The figure above (right) shows LQs for the study group using "adults in poverty" as the denominator (rather than the general population of adults)—in effect controlling for poverty. By controlling for poverty, the number of tracts with substantial concentration (LQ > 2) was reduced and the tracts with elevated LQs (i.e., high concentrations of SMI persons) were more scattered across Philadelphia. They also included areas that did not have an elevated poverty LQ. This more accurately depicted the concentrations and distribution of SMI persons throughout the city.

Results indicated that overall levels of residential segregation among persons with SMI were modest at their most extreme, were not markedly different from a control group of Medicaid recipients without any record of treatment for SMI, and were substantially reduced after taking poverty into account. There were, however, localized areas in Philadelphia that showed distinct concentrations of persons with psychiatric disability, suggesting there may be a subgroup that is more at-risk for living in areas with elevated concentrations of persons with serious psychiatric disability.

EDITING INDIVIDUAL VALUES OR FEATURES

Starting an Edit Session (Step 1)

 From the "**Editor**" toolbar, click the "**Editor**" button and select "**Start Editing**".

You can only edit the contents of one directory at a time in an edit session, so you need to identify the directory that contains the table you wish to edit. You may get a message warning you that the layer's attributes that are about to be edited are in a different coordinate system than the current map's coordinate system. When editing attribute data, this is less of an issue. However, when editing features of the layer, this can—and most likely will—give you unexpected alignment or accuracy problems. It is a good habit to always work with layers that are properly projected.

Editing Attribute Data (Step 2)

Open your attributes table and, using the "Select Elements" tool, click on the cell in your table you wish to edit. When you are finished, go to "Stop Editing" in the edit toolbar and choose "Yes" to save your edits.

FINDING AND REPLACING VALUES

Use the "**Find and Replace**" function to systematically find and replace values in a table.

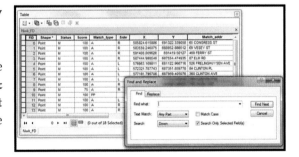

 From the shapefile's attribute table: click the "**Table Options**" button and select "**Find & Replace…**". If you want to replace values, you must start an edit session (from the "**Edit**" toolbar, click the "**Editor**" button and "**Select Editing**").

MEASURING DISTANCE WITH NETWORKS

Euclidean is just one method of measuring distance, and a rather crude one at that. Using Esri's Network Analyst Extension is another method. It lets you factor in travel times and traffic patterns, among other considerations. With the Network Analyst Extension installed and activated: use the "Network Analyst Tools" in ArcToolbox.

CALCULATING AREA, PERIMETER, AND LENGTH

 From the shapefile's attribute table: right-click on the column name where you want to calculate values and select "**Calculate Geometry...**".

Usually there will be fields called "area", "perimeter", and "length" in a shapefile when you receive it that indicates the measures of each map feature. If your shapefile is missing these fields or if you have edited the shape and size of the map features, you will need to calculate them yourself. Area, for example, can be especially helpful when you are trying to normalize values and create densities (e.g. calculating persons per square mile).

For this example, we will calculate "Area," though the process is very similar for the other calculations, as you'll see. You must open the attribute table associated with your shapefile (right click on the name in the table of contents and go to "Open Attribute Table"). From the options menu, go to "Add Field." Call your field "area," choose "double" as the style, and click "OK." Right click on your new field and go to "Calculate Geometry."

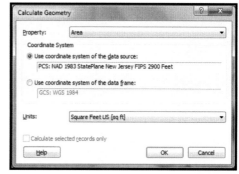

Select the geometric property you want to calculate from the "Property" drop-down menu. Different properties are available depending on the type of layer you're using. To calculate Area, select "Area" from the drop-down menu. To calculate Perimeter, select "Perimeter" from the drop-down menu, etc. Click to use either the coordinate system of the data source or the coordinate system of the data frame. Select the units of the output calculations.

Optionally, if you have selected records in the table, choose whether to apply the calculations to all records or just the selected ones. Finally, click OK.

Tips *(adapted or excerpted from ArcGIS Help files)*

- You can only calculate the area, length, or perimeter of features if the coordinate system being used is projected.
- Keep in mind that different projections have different spatial properties and distortions. If the coordinate system of the data source and data frame are not the same, you may get a different result if you calculate geometry using the data frame's coordinate system than when you calculate using the data source's coordinate system.
- If you are calculating into a text field, you can choose to add a units abbreviation to the calculation. For instance, 47.5673 sq m is an example of the output of area calculated into a text field with the units abbreviation.
- To avoid seeing the warning message when you attempt to calculate values outside an edit session, you can check the Don't warn me again box on the message. You can turn on the warning message again from the Tables tab of the Tools > Options menu.
- The Calculate Geometry dialog box respects the number of decimal places (three, by default) specified on the General tab of the Editing Options dialog box. To change this setting, click the Editor menu on the Editor toolbar and click Options. This setting is saved in the map document.

CHAPTER EIGHT

Working with Shapefiles

EDITING EXISTING SHAPEFILES

Keep in mind that editing shapefiles can change attribute values (such as area and perimeter) that you may need to update.

 From the Standard toolbar: click "**Customize**", select "**Toolbars**" and activate "**Editor**".

Deleting and Modifying Features

You must start an edit session to make changes to a shapefile.

From the Editor toolbar: choose "**Start Editing**." Or, from the Table of Contents in ArcMap: right-click the layer you wish to edit, click "**Edit Features**" and select "**Start Editing**"

If you have multiple shapefiles in your ArcMap document that are from different directories on your computer, you must specify which directory will be part of the edit session (you can only edit the files in one directory at a time). You may want to make a backup of your original data before editing.

 From the Target drop down menu in the Editor toolbar: indicate which map layer you wish to edit. Use the "**Edit**" tool to click on the feature (point, line, polygon) you wish to edit (it should become highlighted). By clicking and holding down the mouse button, you can move your map feature to a new location. To modify a line or polygon feature, double click on it. Notice that the vertices become visible and the Task menu automatically brings up **"Edit Vertices."** You can reshape your feature by putting your cursor over a vertex, clicking, and dragging it. Click outside of the map feature to complete. (ArcMap will show the last created vertex in red). You can **"Insert Vertex"** to a feature by right clicking on a green line and going to "Insert vertex" (a new vertex will be created where you right click). Click anywhere on the map to confirm the edits. You can delete a vertex by placing your cursor over the vertex, right-clicking, and choosing "**Delete Vertex**." To save edits, from the Editor menu on the Editor toolbar, choose "**Stop Editing**" and choose "Yes" to save edits. Notice that you do not have a "Save As..." option.

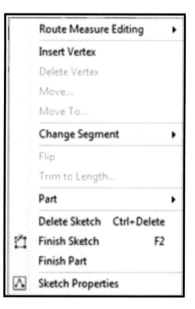

Advanced Edit Tools

There are several advanced editing tools.

 From ArcMap: go to **"Customize"**, click "Toolbars" and select "**Advanced Editing**".

Edit Tasks

The "**Editor**" drop-down list on the Editor toolbar contains a set of editing tasks that affects how the Sketch tool functions. Additional tools can be found on the toolbar as icons. The editing tasks are organized into four groups: Create Tasks, Modify Tasks, Topology Tasks, and Other Tasks. For example: to **split features** (i.e. to cut a polygon into two new polygons) select the polygon you want to cut, choose the Cut Polygon Features task, then use the Sketch tool to define the line along which you want to cut the selected polygon.

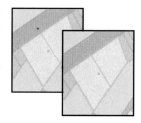

Merging Features

The "**Merge**" tool combines input datasets of the same data type into a single, composite dataset.

 From the Standard toolbar: click "**Geoprocessing**" and activate the "**Merge**" tool. **Or, from ArcToolbox:** click "**Data Management**", select "**General**" and activate "**Merge**".

Once the "Merge" dialog window is open:

 Add the layers you wish to merge in "**Input Datasets**". Create a name and location for the "**Output Dataset**". Identify the fields chosen from the inputs in "**Field Map**", if necessary.

You can also merge datasets without having to open the "Merge" tool as well:

 In order to dissolve the boundaries between two or more polygon features, you must start an edit session. Using the edit tool and the shift key, click on the features you wish to merge (they should become highlighted), then from the Editor menu on the Editor toolbar select "**Merge**..." You can also select map features based on their attributes by opening the attribute table and selecting the corresponding records.

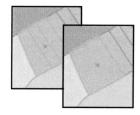

Intersecting Features

The "**Intersect**" command creates a new feature from the common areas or edges of any two selected features of the same geometry type. For instance, you can create a new patrol area out of overlapping patrol areas. The original features are maintained, and the new feature is created in the target layer without attribute values (they can be entered manually).

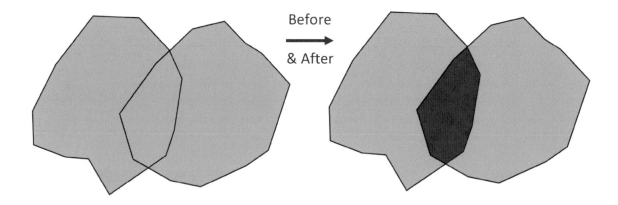

The Intersect Geoprocessing Tool creates new features from the overlaps of all input layers or feature classes. You can create a new feature from the intersection of features of different layers, but the layers must be of the same geometry type (either line or polygon). Line features that you are trying to intersect must share a common edge. Two lines that cross each other, such as in an X pattern, do not share a common edge; To

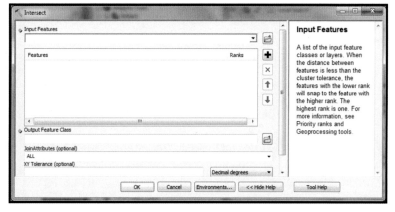

break this type of line intersection, you must use the "Split" command on the Editor toolbar.

 From the Standard toolbar: click "**Geoprocessing**" and activate the "**Intersect**" tool. **Or, From ArcToolbox**: click "**Analysis Tools**" and select "**Intersect**".

Once you have activated the "Intersect" tool:

 From the "**Input Features**" dropdown menu: select the layers you wish to intersect. You will notice that you are able to rank the layers with the features of the lower rank snapping onto the feature of the higher rank. You can also choose what attributes from the input features will be transferred to the features of the output shapefile.

ADDING OTHER GRAPHICS

ArcMap has a set of tools on the Drawing toolbar used to create graphics. Objects drawn with the drawing tools are stored in the map document as graphic images, not as features in a feature class (and they have no attributes attached to them).

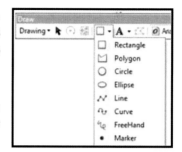

 To access the "**Draw**" toolbar: click "**Customize**", select "**Toolbars**", and activate "**Draw**". From the Drawing toolbar, click any of the drawing tools (as shown to the right) and draw graphics.

CREATING NEW SHAPEFILES

If you need a line or polygon file that does not exist—such as a boundary for your study area—you will need to create it yourself. Digitizing is the process of drawing or tracing map features to create a new geographic file. ArcMap has some digitizing tools that allow you to create new shapefiles without additional hardware or software.

 From ArcCatalog: right-click the folder where the new shapefile will be stored, click "**New**" and select "**Shapefile...**". From the "**Create New Shapefile**" dialog box, give your new shapefile a name and indicate what **"Feature Type"** the shapefile will have: point, line, or polygon. Use the "**Edit**..." button to set the projection. This shapefile is essentially just a shell since it contains no information. But you need this before you can start to create new map features. Next, open ArcMap and add your new shapefile, along with other map layers that may serve as references to help you draw your new features. Start an edit session (i.e., from the Editor menu in the "**Editor**" toolbar, choose "**Start Editing**") and indicate which directory contains the shapefile (shell) you just created. Be sure that your new shapefile is listed as the "**Target**" in the "Editor" toolbar and that "**Create New Features**" is selected from the "Task" menu. Choose a drawing/construction tool to begin digitizing.

Using the Drawing/Construction Tools

Click to create a new vertex, click again to create another vertex, etc. Right-click and click "**Finish Sketch**" to finish. To delete the newly-created feature, click on it using the Edit Tool to select it and then hit the Delete key on your keyboard. Hit Ctrl+Z to undo the last vertex. To save your new feature, from the Editor menu choose "Stop Editing" and save edits.

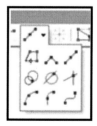

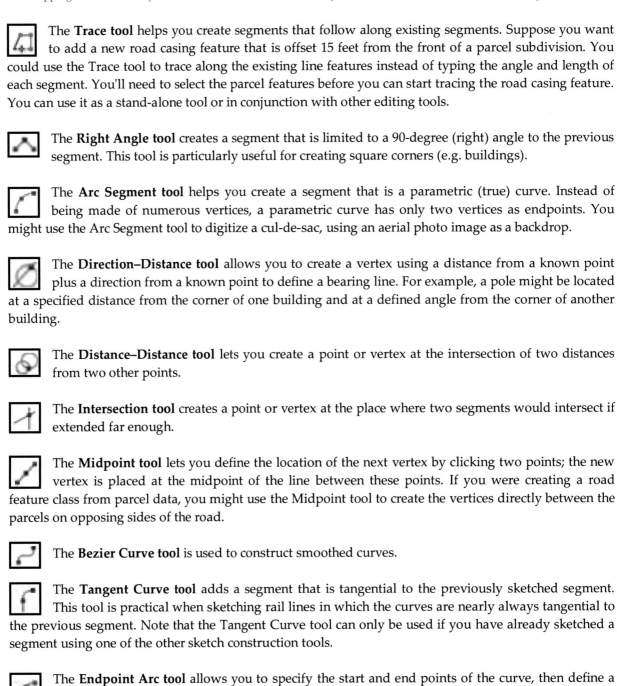

The **Trace tool** helps you create segments that follow along existing segments. Suppose you want to add a new road casing feature that is offset 15 feet from the front of a parcel subdivision. You could use the Trace tool to trace along the existing line features instead of typing the angle and length of each segment. You'll need to select the parcel features before you can start tracing the road casing feature. You can use it as a stand-alone tool or in conjunction with other editing tools.

The **Right Angle tool** creates a segment that is limited to a 90-degree (right) angle to the previous segment. This tool is particularly useful for creating square corners (e.g. buildings).

The **Arc Segment tool** helps you create a segment that is a parametric (true) curve. Instead of being made of numerous vertices, a parametric curve has only two vertices as endpoints. You might use the Arc Segment tool to digitize a cul-de-sac, using an aerial photo image as a backdrop.

The **Direction–Distance tool** allows you to create a vertex using a distance from a known point plus a direction from a known point to define a bearing line. For example, a pole might be located at a specified distance from the corner of one building and at a defined angle from the corner of another building.

The **Distance–Distance tool** lets you create a point or vertex at the intersection of two distances from two other points.

The **Intersection tool** creates a point or vertex at the place where two segments would intersect if extended far enough.

The **Midpoint tool** lets you define the location of the next vertex by clicking two points; the new vertex is placed at the midpoint of the line between these points. If you were creating a road feature class from parcel data, you might use the Midpoint tool to create the vertices directly between the parcels on opposing sides of the road.

The **Bezier Curve tool** is used to construct smoothed curves.

The **Tangent Curve tool** adds a segment that is tangential to the previously sketched segment. This tool is practical when sketching rail lines in which the curves are nearly always tangential to the previous segment. Note that the Tangent Curve tool can only be used if you have already sketched a segment using one of the other sketch construction tools.

The **Endpoint Arc tool** allows you to specify the start and end points of the curve, then define a radius for the curve. This is particularly useful when sketching cul-de-sacs, where the beginning and ending points of the arc, as well as the radius of the cul-de-sac, are known.

Use the **Sketch tool** to create point features and digitize the vertices of line or polygon features. After you finish the sketch, ArcMap adds the final segment, and the sketch turns into a feature.

You can also take advantage of the "**Feature Construction**" mini-toolbar. This mini-toolbar becomes active when you start sketching. The mini-toolbar is semi-transparent when you are working with your map; it becomes opaque when you begin using it.

Create Features Window

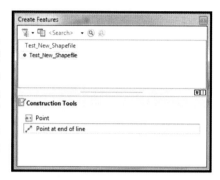

The "**Create Features**" window combines the "**Target Layer**", "**Sketch**" tools and the "**Task List**" from previous versions of ArcMap. The window operates in a template format. Templates have a specific name, description, and purpose. Additionally, each template has default tools (located within the "**Construction Tools**" panel). As there may not be a template for all of your needs, a template is automatically created for each layer within the current editing workspace.

Snapping to an Existing Feature

It is nearly impossible to draw features that match an existing layer just by looking at it. Snapping to features of an existing shapefile allows you to create new features that match the reference map layer exactly—without overlaps or gaps.

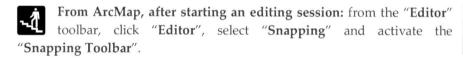

From ArcMap, after starting an editing session: from the "Editor" toolbar, click "**Editor**", select "**Snapping**" and activate the "**Snapping Toolbar**".

From the Editor menu on the Editor toolbar, go to Start Editing and indicate which directory contains the shapefile (shell) to which you want to add map features. At the top of the "Snapping Environment" options box, you can identify the layer(s) to which you want to snap your new features. If you use a street centerline file as your guide, vertices will work well.

To create the most accurate line, move your cursor slowly over the existing shapefile, clicking at each vertex to create a new vertex in your shapefile. You can change the snapping "Tolerance"—the distance from the existing shapefile you can be and still snap to it—from the Editor menu: choose "**Options**," and go to "**Tolerance**". The map units reflect the units you identified in the Data Frame properties (General tab).

Using the snapping tool, you should be able to create new features that line up exactly with existing shapefiles. If you are not happy with your results, click on the map feature with the Edit tool and hit "**Delete**" (you can do this even after saving edits to the shapefile, as long as you start an Edit Session).

Adding Attribute Data to New Features

After creating new features in a new shapefile (or after editing/adding features in an existing shapefile), you can assign information to them in the Attributes table. Attribute tables of new shapefiles with new features will have only three columns named FID, Shape, and ID. These are automatically created by ArcMap.

 From the Table of Contents: right-click the new layer and select "**Open Attribute Table...**". Click and select "**Add Field...**". If you are unable to select this option, go back to the Editor toolbar, click "**Stop Editing**", and then try again to add a field (You cannot add fields during an edit session). Once the new field has (or many fields have) been added, click "**Editor**" on the Editor toolbar, and then "**Start Editing**". Be sure to save your edits!

To add a new field(s) to an Attribute table, you <u>cannot</u> be in an edit session. But, in order to type data into the fields of an Attribute table, you <u>must</u> be in an edit session.

CHAPTER NINE

ArcToolbox and Geoprocessing

BUFFERS

Buffer functionality allows you to create temporary graphics or permanent shapefiles around existing map features. You can create buffers around any type of vector data (points, line, or polygons) and around selected or all features in a map layer. The Buffer tool is readily accessible through the Data View; however, you may also use ArcToolbox to open the Buffer tool and the Multiple Ring Buffer tool.

Buffer Tool

 From the Standard toolbar: click "**Geoprocessing**" and select "**Buffer**". Click 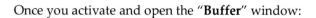 on the Tools toolbar, click "**Analysis Tools**", select "**Proximity**" and activate "**Buffer**".

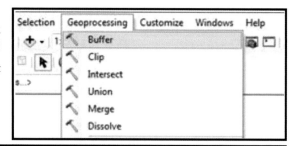

Once you activate and open the "**Buffer**" window:

Select the feature/layer you wish to create a buffer within the "**Input Features**" dropdown menu. Create an output name and location. Input the distance or length of the buffer within "**Linear unit**". You can also create a buffer based on a map attribute. Make sure to select the appropriate unit from the dropdown beside the "**Linear unit**". Edit "**Side Type**", "**End Type**" and "**Dissolve Type**" as you see fit.

Multiple Ring Buffer Tool

The "**Multiple Ring Buffer**" tool creates concentric buffers.

 Click 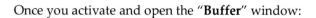 on the Data view interface, click "**Analysis Tools**", select "**Proximity**" and activate "**Multiple Ring Buffer**".

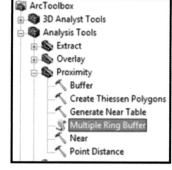

Once you activate and open the "**Multiple Ring Buffer**" tool:

 Select the feature/layer you wish to create a buffer within the "**Input Features**" dropdown menu. Create an output name and location. Input the distance or length of the buffers within "**Distances**". Make sure to select the appropriate unit from the "**Buffer Unit**" dropdown menu.

Buffering can take ArcMap a long time, especially if you choose to dissolve the barriers within the buffers. However, if you do not dissolve the barriers, your buffers may involve lots of separate polygons. If you save the buffers as a shapefile, there will be an attribute table with records corresponding to the separate polygons making up the buffer. If you choose to dissolve the barriers, there will be fewer (or possible just one record/polygon).

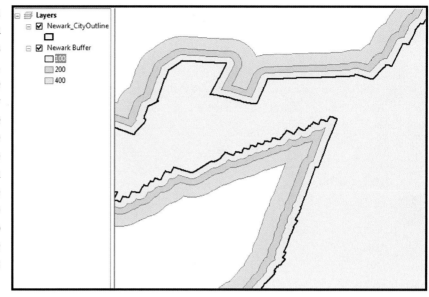

ARCTOOLBOX WINDOW

 From ArcMap or ArcCatalog: click the "**ArcToolbox**" icon (see left).

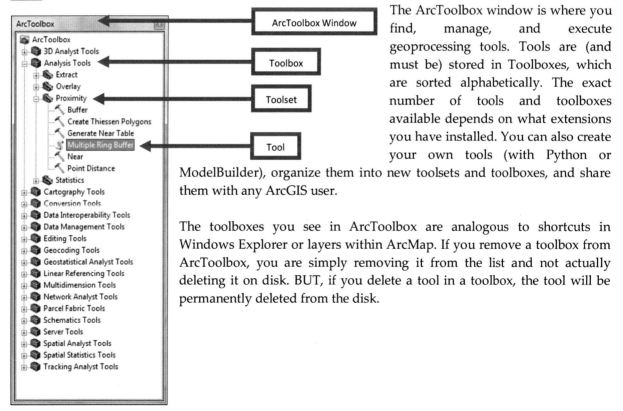

The ArcToolbox window is where you find, manage, and execute geoprocessing tools. Tools are (and must be) stored in Toolboxes, which are sorted alphabetically. The exact number of tools and toolboxes available depends on what extensions you have installed. You can also create your own tools (with Python or ModelBuilder), organize them into new toolsets and toolboxes, and share them with any ArcGIS user.

The toolboxes you see in ArcToolbox are analogous to shortcuts in Windows Explorer or layers within ArcMap. If you remove a toolbox from ArcToolbox, you are simply removing it from the list and not actually deleting it on disk. BUT, if you delete a tool in a toolbox, the tool will be permanently deleted from the disk.

Docking and Undocking

 You can dock the "**ArcToolbox**" window by double-clicking the bar at the top of the window. To undock, simply double-click the window once docked.

You can move the ArcToolbox window by clicking on the bar at the top and dragging it. The window can be docked—like the Table of Contents, or you can undock the window to have it float above the application by double-clicking the window bar and vice-versa to undock. This is the same procedure for all the tool windows in ArcMap.

Opening Tools

 From the "ArcToolbox" window: double-click the tool.

Search Tool

If you know, generally, the name of the tool you want to use or the function you want to perform, but cannot remember where the tool is located, use the "Search" tab.

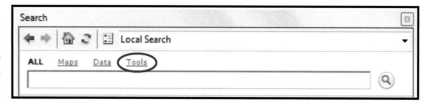

 Click the "**Search window**" icon (see left) on the Data view interface, type in the keyword(s) and click the "Search" button. To help limit the search to tools, click the "**Tools**" option. Results will appear in the box below. Click the tool to activate.

⚠ *When you search a particular tool, it will provide the tool icon, tool name and tool summary. Additionally, the results will provide the 'address' of the tool underneath the tool summary (see below).*

Toolbox = analysis tools
Toolset = proximity
Tool = buffer

MODEL BUILDER

ModelBuilder is a tool that helps you build, manage and automate spatial models. A spatial model is a set of one or more processes. A process includes input data, a spatial function (tool) that operates on the input data, and output data. Processes can be connected so that the output of one process becomes the input to another process.

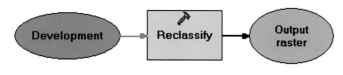

A spatial model is represented in ModelBuilder as a diagram that looks like a flowchart. The spatial model does not actually contain spatial data; it has placeholders, called nodes, which represent the data that is processed and created when the model is run. The nodes are connected by arrows that show the sequence of processing in the model. The actual data is managed and displayed in ArcMap; ModelBuilder just gives processing instructions to ArcMap when the model is run. To build a new model, start by opening ArcMap and add one or more existing data layers that will be used as input to the model you are about to build.

 Click the "**Modelbuilder window**" icon.

Detailed steps for using ModelBuilder to build a model are not discussed here. For more information refer to the ArcGIS Desktop Help.

ModelBuilder Tips

- Use Model > Run Entire Model
- To save a model, use Model > Save
- To close a model, use Model > Close or just close the ModelBuilder window.
- To rename a model, right-click on its name in the ArcToolbox > Rename
- To open a saved model for editing, right-click on its name in ArcToolbox > Edit

---

SPATIAL DATA PROCESSING TOOLS

Transforming Shapefiles

There are a number of different functions you can perform on map layers, either based on location or attribute value that result in new map layers. In ArcMap 10, they have been incorporated into an expanded suite of data management tools. You must define the projection for map layers before using any of these functions. If you selected a subset of features within a map layer, the functions will only be performed on the selected features.

Examples of the tools described in this section are below:

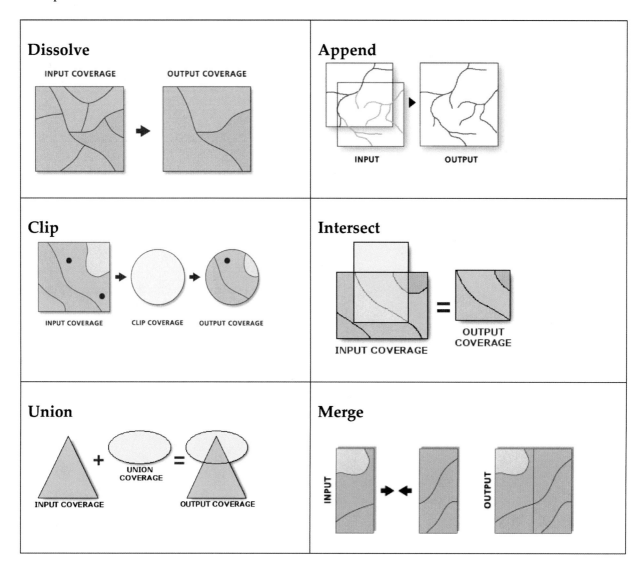

ArcMap 10 has made it easier for users to access most of these tools (except "**Append**", but including "**Buffer**") within the "**Geoprocessing**" tab in the Standard toolbar.

 *The following screen captures of the tool windows will have the "**Help**" option activated (on the right side of the window). To deactivate, click the "<< **Hide Help**".*

Dissolve

The dissolve operation allows you to collapse the boundaries between polygons if they share the same value on a particular attribute. For example, you could create a neighborhood map layer by assigning each blockgroup to a neighborhood and then dissolving the boundaries.

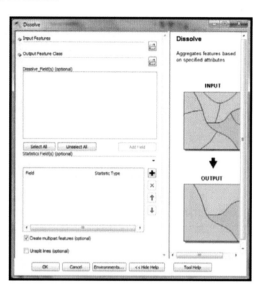

From ArcToolbox: click "**Data Management Tools**", select "**Generalization**" and activate the "**Dissolve**" tool. **Or, From the Standard toolbar**: click "**Geoprocessing**" and select "**Dissolve**".

Once you have activated the "Dissolve" tool, you can begin:

You need to identify the map layer whose features you wish to dissolve under "**Input Features**". Provide a name for the new shapefile and location under "**Output Feature Class**" (otherwise ArcMap will provide a default name by adding "_Dissolve" to the original name). Choose the column/field(s) you wish to dissolve in the "**Dissolve_Field(s)**" section. This must be an attribute for which multiple map features (polygons) have the exact same value.

⚠ *The values can be numbers or text, although keep in mind that nominal and categorical variables will work better than ratio variables. If polygons have the same value but are not contiguous, they will still be dissolved into a "multipart feature."*

Append

Appending allows you to incorporate two or more non-overlapping layers into a single map layer without changing their map features. You can append point, line, and polygon layers. Appending can save you time when it comes to symbolizing features and can lead to more consistent symbology. For example, you can append (i.e. merge) census tract files from several counties so that when you display the percent of homeowners, you do not have to repeat the process of classifying your data for each county.

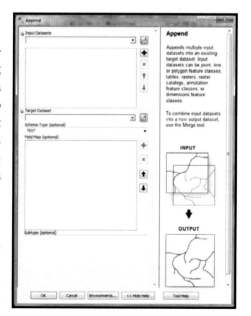

From ArcToolbox: click "**Data Management Tools**", select "**General**" and activate the "**Append**". Under "**Input Datasets**", list all the map layers you wish to merge. Under "**Target Dataset**", specify an EXISTING layer as a new layer will NOT be automatically created. This will overwrite the existing layer, so be sure to make a backup copy, if necessary. If the columns in the attribute tables of all the input features are identical, you can select "**TEST**" under "**Schema Type**". Otherwise, you must choose "**NO_TEST**".

The resulting shapefile will contain all of the map features in the appended layers. Keep in mind that these merged shapefiles can grow very large, particularly if you merge street centerline files.

Clip

Clipping allows you to turn one shapefile into a cookie-cutter in order to cut out part of another shapefile. Essentially, the "**Clip**" tool allows you to clip *vector* shapefiles. For example, you might need to create a map layer of streets for the area within a single police district but your street centerline file covers the entire city. Using a street file that is clipped by the police district boundary will allow you to work with a smaller and more manageable file that looks neater.

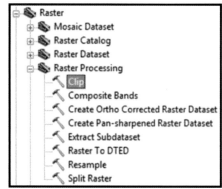

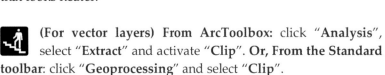 (For vector layers) From ArcToolbox: click "**Analysis**", select "**Extract**" and activate "**Clip**". Or, From the Standard toolbar: click "**Geoprocessing**" and select "**Clip**".

Once you have activated the "Clip" tool, you may begin:

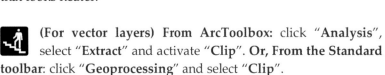 In "**Clip**" dialog box, you need to identify an "**Input Feature**" (the layer to be clipped) and the "**Clip Features**" (cookie cutter). Specify the name and location of the new file in the "**Output Feature Class**" field. You can leave "**XY Tolerance**" blank, or at 0. Changing it will allow slightly mismatched map layers to be considered "coincident."

You can also clip raster grids by using a raster clipping tool:

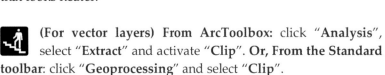 (For raster grids) From ArcToolbox: click "**Data Management Tools**", select "**Raster**" and click "**Raster Processing**". Activate "**Clip**". Proceed in a similar fashion as the vector clip, but make sure you provide the "**Rectangle**" coordinates or if you want to clip the raster based on the polygon features within the shapefile, check the box next to "**Use Input Features for Clipping Geometry**".

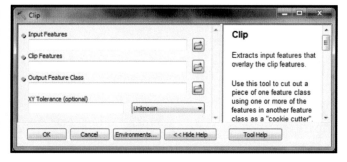

As with any tool, you can also find vector and raster clipping tools by searching for the keyword "clip" using the "**Search window**". Double-clicking on the tool in the results area opens it directly.

Intersect

Intersect allows you to fuse two overlapping layers together to create a new shapefile that includes the attributes of both layers for the area in which the layers overlap. In effect, this combines the union (described below) and clip operations. You can intersect two polygon layers or a line and polygon layer.

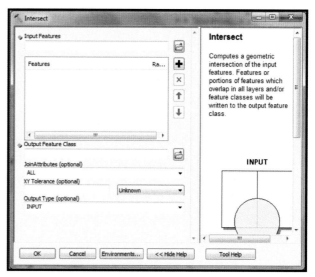

From the ArcToolbox: click **"Analysis Tools"**, select **"Overlay"** and activate **"Intersect"**. **Or, From the Standard toolbar**: click **"Geoprocessing"** and select **"Intersect"**.

Once you activated the "Intersect" tool, you may begin:

In the "**Intersect**" window, select "**Input Features**". The default name for the new shapefile will be the first input feature name plus "_Intersect". If you want to change this or the location of the new file, click on the folder to the right of the "**Output Feature Class**" field.

If you intersect a line and polygon layers, the resulting shapefile will contain "polylines" that act like lines. If you intersect polygon layers, the resulting shapefile will contain polygons. Length, perimeter, and area values will be inaccurate after you perform an intersection, so if you need these be sure to recalculate them. Other attribute values may be deceptive, as well.

Union

Union is similar to intersection in that it fuses the boundaries of two layers together, but rather than clipping the resulting shapefile to include only the area covered by both, it creates a new shapefile that covers the combined extent of the layers.

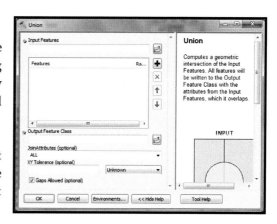

From the ArcToolbox: click "**Analysis Tools**", select "**Overlay**" and activate "**Union**". **Or, From the Standard toolbar**: click "**Geoprocessing**" and select "**Union**".

Once you activate the "**Union**" tool, you may begin:

Select the "**Input Features**". The default name for the new shapefile will be the first input feature name plus "_Union." If you want to change this or the location of the new file, click on the folder to the right of the "**Output Feature Class**" field. As with shapefiles created through intersections, the shapefiles

created by a union will most likely have some attribute values that no longer make sense. Be sure to recalculate length, perimeter, and area if you need these variables.

Merge

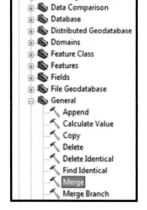

Merge is similar to "Dissolve". However, while the Dissolve tool combines features within the same shapefile based on a common attribute, the Merge tool combines features from multiple sources/shapefiles into a single, new, output shapefile. The features must all be the same type (i.e. point, line, polygon). The "Merge" tool keeps all of the input features as separate entities. The input features do not have to be adjacent, overlap or distance between features is allowed.

 From the ArcToolbox: click "**Data Management Tools**", select "**General**" and activate "**Merge**". **Or, From the Standard toolbar**: click "**Geoprocessing**" and select "**Merge**".

Once you have activated the "**Merge**" tool, you may begin:

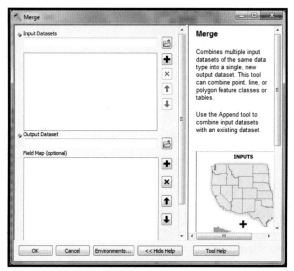

 Select all of the input datasets that you want to combine together within "**Input Datasets**". These can be point, line, or polygon feature classes; tables can also be merged. In the "**Output Dataset**" text box, specify a name and location the new shapefile that will be created. For the "**Field Map**" option, you can specifically choose the fields you want to incorporate from the inputs. You also have the ability to create new fields.

Create Random Points

This tool does just what it says—it creates a specified number of random points within polygons or along line features of a shapefile. The placement of points is done according to specialized algorithms that consider the geography of the extent where the points can lay. Remember, "random" does not mean "mutually exclusive." So, at least conceivably, two or more points can be placed at the same location; this is rare, but the probability does exist. It is always a good habit to review the placement of points after they are created to ensure that they will satisfy your needs.

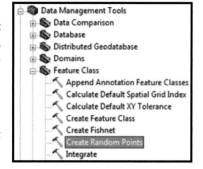

 From the ArcToolbox: click "**Data Management Tools**", select "**Feature Class**" and activate the "**Create Random Points**" tool.

Once you have activated the "Create Random Points" tool, you may begin:

The "**Output Location**" text box requires you to select an existing folder (i.e. directory) where the new shapefile with random points will be created. Provide a name for the random points in the "**Outpoint Point Feature Class**" text box. The "**Constraining Feature Class**" or "**Constraining Extent**" options are useful if you want to limit the possible locations of points to a specific study area (i.e. extent) or within/along features of an existing shapefile. The number of points to be randomly assigned can be specified as a long integer number or as a field and is placed within the "**Long**" or "**Field**" text boxes. You can also include a "**Minimum Allowed Distance**", either a "**Linear unit**" or "**Field**" for your random points. Lastly, you can also choose a multipoint input by checking the "**Create Multipoint Outpoint**" box.

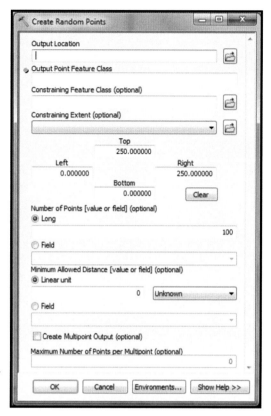

When you "constrain" points to features, ArcMap places the specified number points to every unique feature. With a shapefile of streets, for example, which tends to have many line segments, 10 points will be randomly placed on every line segment if you specify "10" as the value in the "Number of Points" text box. To create 10 random points throughout the entire street network, "dissolve" the street segments to create a single polyline feature for use as the "Constraining Feature Class".

CHAPTER TEN

Raster Data Analysis and Mapping

SPATIAL ANALYST EXTENSION

The Spatial Analyst Extension is specifically intended for the processing of grids (raster data). You will need it to make density maps and work with raster data. Accessing the extension requires up to 3 steps.

1. Install and Register the Spatial Analyst Extension

Whether you have a trial version or a full license of ArcGIS, you will need to install and register the Spatial Analyst Extension.

2. Activate the Spatial Analyst Extension

Once extensions are installed and registered, you need to activate them in ArcView.

 Open ArcMap and from the Standard toolbar: click **"Customize"** and select **"Extensions..."**. Check the **"Spatial Analyst"** box.

⚠ *This is also how you would activate other extensions, including 3D Analyst and Network Analyst.*

If you attempt to use a "Spatial Analyst" tool and do not have the extension activated or the license has not been registered, a window will appear that states "Tool Not Licensed".

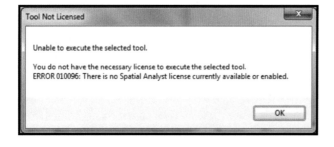

3. Display the Spatial Analyst Toolbar

 From ArcMap: click **"Customize"** on the Standard toolbar and click **"Spatial Analyst"**.

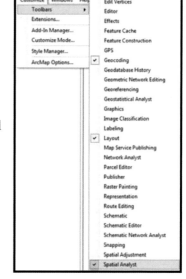

The Spatial Analyst Toolbar looks like this:

Unlike the "Spatial Analyst" toolbar in the previous version of ArcGIS, there are only two interactive tools located within the toolbar in ArcMap 10: the "**Create Contour**" and the "**Histogram**" tools. The "Create Contour" tool allows you to create independent contours (lines that connect cells of equal value). The "Histogram" tool allows you to assess the distribution of values within a raster layer. Both tools only become activated when an appropriate map layer is included within ArcMap's Table of Contents.

Using Spatial Analyst in ArcToolbox

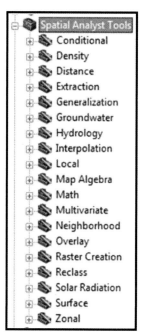

As with many of the tools and applications, ArcToolbox is vital for using "Spatial Analyst" tools and will be the main way for you to access the tools.

 From the ArcToolbox: click "**Spatial Analyst Tools**" and double-click the tool you want to use.

You have a plethora (yes, plethora) of toolsets within the "Spatial Analyst" toolbox. We will only discuss a few of them here, so it may be worthwhile for you to familiarize yourself with the others on your own.

DENSITY RASTER MAPPING

There are three types of "**Density**" maps you can create in ArcMap 10: "**Kernel Density**", "**Line Density**" and "**Point Density**".

Kernel Density calculates the magnitude per unit area from a specific point or polyline using a kernel function. Conceptually, a smooth curved surface is fitted over each point feature. The surface value is highest at the location of the point, and diminishes with increasing distance from the point, reaching zero at search radius distance from the point. This is the tool most often used for "hotspot" density mapping.

Line Density calculates a magnitude per unit area from polyline features that fall within a specific radius around each cell within the map.

Point Density calculates a magnitude per unit area from point features that fall within a neighborhood around each cell. Conceptually, a neighborhood is defined around each raster cell center, and the number of points that fall within the neighborhood is totaled and divided by the area of the neighborhood.

Since "**Kernel Density**" is most likely the density tool you will use in most cases, we will specifically dedicate this section to it; however, many of the steps are applicable for "Line" and "Point" density tools as well.

 From the ArcToolbox: click "**Spatial Analyst Tools**" and select "**Kernel Density**". In the "**Kernel Density**" dialog box, select the "**Input point or polyline features**" to calculate density from. The "**Population field**" is the quantity that is to be used in the calculation of, or that is spread across the landscape to create, a continuous surface. Use "NONE" if no item or special value will be used and each feature will be counted once. Choose an appropriate "**Output cell size**" (size of individual cells in the output raster) and "**Search radius**" (determines how generalized the density patterns will appear) or leave as the default. Lastly, make sure that the "**Area units**" is the unit you wish to use as it determines how the density values will be calculated. If the map units are known (i.e. projected), then Area Units can be Square Miles, Square Kilometers, Acres, Hectares, Square Yards, Square Inches, Square Meters, Square Centimeters, or Square Millimeters.

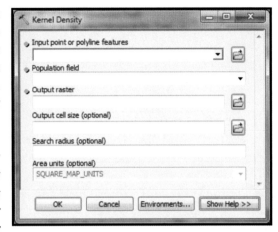

⚠ *When determining the "**Output cell size**", remember that the smaller the cell size, the smoother the density will be. However, very small cells also require more processing time and computer storage space. Additionally, a smaller "**Search radius**", will show more local variation, while a larger search radius will show broader patterns in the data.*

Possible Error When Calculating Density of Geocoded Points

You might receive an error message when attempting to calculate the density of points that were geocoded with a match rate below 100%. The cause of the error is likely that there are "unmatched" addresses that appear in the shapefile's attribute table. Because the addresses are unmatched, there are no respective points on the map. This presents a problem to ArcMap when it cannot find these points to include in the density calculation. To

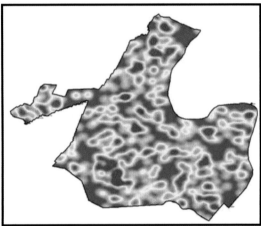

resolve this quickly, you must create a new shapefile with only the "Matched" or "Tied" records, thereby removing the "unmatched" records from the shapefile and its attribute table. Or, if you want a more inclusive density map with all of the original records, you must clean the data and geocode it properly.

To remove unmatched records from an existing shapefile:
In the Attributes table, there is a column called "Status" that notes whether each record was Matched (M), Tied (T), or Unmatched (U) during the geocoding process. Select all of the "M" and "T" records and then export these selected data to create a new shapefile (i.e. without unmatched records). Perform a density calculation using this new shapefile as the "Input data".

Density Map Symbology

From the Table of Contents in ArcMap: right-click the layer (raster map) you want to work with, click "**Properties**" and select the "**Symbology**" tab.

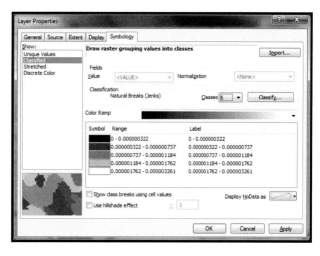

Symbolizing raster (i.e. density) maps differs slightly from vector maps. By default, density map symbology is displayed as "**Equal Interval**".

⚠ *You may get a message that says "Unique histogram does not exist. Do you want to compute unique values?" Click "Yes".*

In the "**Layer Properties**" dialog box, under the "**Symbology**" tab, click the "**Classify**..." button under the "**Classified**" scheme. Standard Deviation (SD) is a good option for showing variation in raster values. The map on the left in the example (to the right) shows a "**Stretched**" classification scheme, whereby each cell is shaded from white to black according to its density value. In this map, darker colored cells represent a higher density of gang member residences.

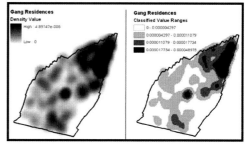

The map on the right shows the same cells classified into four groups—according to SD breaks. White colored cells have values below the mean cell value; cells colored light grey have values between the mean and +1 standard deviation (SD); cells colored dark grey have values between +1 SD and +2 SD; cells colored black have values greater than +2 SD. In other words, the black colored cells have values in the top five percent of the distribution (remember the 68-95-99.7 rule from statistics?).

SYMBOLIZING RASTER DENSITY MAPS WITH MULTIPLE LAYERS

It can be difficult to symbolize a density raster map in a way that makes another map layer below it easily visible. For example, you could make the top raster map partially transparent to see through it to the layer below (as demonstrated in the figure to the right). However, this can be confusing to the map reader and it tends to print to paper much worse than it appears on a computer screen.

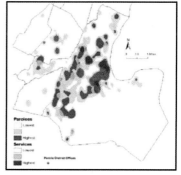

Transparency works best with color raster maps, but should be used cautiously and sparingly, and only after careful consideration has been given to the map's intended purpose and the medium by which the final map will be delivered (i.e. computer screen or printed document). Colors and transparency are not appropriate for black-and-white publishing (e.g. journal articles) or for documents that will likely be copied and distributed widely (e.g. policy briefs).

Converting raster maps to vector features (such as polygons) provides additional symbology options, particularly in grayscale. For example, the figure to the right communicates the same information as the color map (above), but does so in grayscale and with the "Social Services Density" layer converted from raster to polygonal features. This allows for the crosshatching that symbolizes the "Highest" density areas. Layering these raster and vector maps permits a clearer visual analysis of the spatial overlap of parolee residences and social services. While parolees may live on any piece of land in Newark (with the exclusion of the Newark International Airport or the seaport), a higher concentration of parolees live in the shaded grey areas on the map; a higher concentration of social services are located within the black outlines and crosshatched areas on the map.

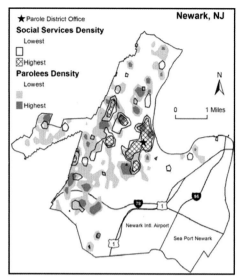

Before converting a raster map to polygonal features, you should symbolize it using the "Classified" schema. The "Classified" schema groups raster cells based on their respective values, and then symbolizes them accordingly. For example, the raster map to the right is classified into four categories: All raster cells whose numerical values are above +2 Standard Deviations (SD) are symbolized with the color Black. All raster cells whose numerical values are between +1 SD and +2 SD are symbolized with the Medium Grey color; between the Mean and +1 SD is Light Grey; less than the Mean is White. Each

raster cell retains its original value; it is merely (temporarily) symbolized according to a four category classification schema. You can then convert the similarly grouped contiguous cells into polygonal features. First, however, you must permanently change the values of the cells to specify to which group they belong. For example, all cells whose original values are above +2 SD (symbolized by the color Black) will get a new value of "4"; all cells whose original values are between +1 SD and +2 SD will get a new value of "3"; and so on. This task is done using the "**Reclassify**" operation in the Spatial Analyst Extenstion.

RECLASSIFY RASTER VALUES

A raster map is a grid of equally-sized cells covering the entire study area. Each cell has only one value associated with it. The Reclassify operation changes the values. This can be used to generalize or create new categories of data, or to create discrete categories from continuous data (such as density values).

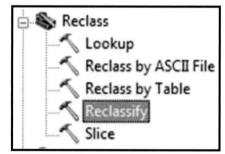

 From ArcToolbox: click "**Spatial Analyst Tools**", select "**Reclass**" and activate "**Reclassify**".

Once you have activated the "Reclassify" tool, you can begin to reclassify your raster map:

In the "**Input Raster**" field of the "Reclassify" window, select the raster map whose values you want to permanately change. ("Reclassify" actually creates a new raster layer, so the original raster map and data will not be altered). Notice how the "**Old values**" are grouped into the same classification schema that the map is symbolized in. By default, the "**New values**" are ordered numerically (e.g. from 1 to 4). Manually enter new values for each category or keep the defaults. New values can be of the numerical or string type. Choose a name and location to save the "**Output raster**" and then click the "OK" button. A new raster map will be created: In this example, each cell will have a value of either 1, 2, 3 or 4. For your convenience, you can also define the classification of your raster map by clicking the "**Classify...**" button from within the "Reclassify" window.

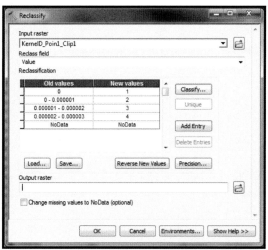

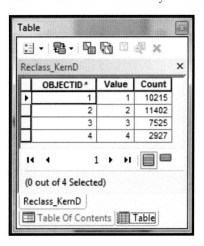

The Attribute table of the new (Reclassified) raster map shows that 10,215 cells now have the value of "1", 11,402 cells have the value "2", and so on (see left). Groups of contiguous cells with the same values can now be converted into polygonal features using a "**Convert**" tool.

RASTER/VECTOR CONVERSIONS

Unlike the tools discussed above, conversion tools are not located within the "Spatial Analyst Tools" toolset; however, for continuity purposes, we shall incorporate them here. Conversion tools ("Convert") were formerly part of the "Spatial Analyst" toolbar in ArcGIS 9.3.

In ArcMap 10, conversion tools are given their own toolbox named "**Conversion Tools**". Simply put, conversion tools can be used to convert your map surfaces into different formats. This is particularly beneficial if you want to conduct different analyses (i.e. in programs other than ArcGIS or using different data types). While we will not discuss all the available

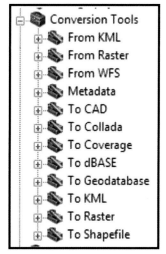

conversion tools, it may be in your best interest to get an idea of what is available and what they can do.

From ArcToolbox: click "**Conversion Tools**", select the toolset you wish to use and activate the tool.

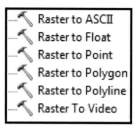

For our purposes, we will focus our attention on the "**From Raster**" and "**To Raster**" toolsets. As discussed in the last section, groups of contiguous cells with the same values can now be converted into polygonal features using a "Convert" tool. Since we are working *from* a raster format, we will use the "**From Raster**" toolset. The "From Raster" toolset offers several tools (see right). However, we are especially interested in the "**…to Point**", "**…to Polygon**" and "**…to Polyline**" tools.

 From ArcToolbox: click "**Convsersion Tools**", select "**From Raster**" and choose one of the three tools (we display the "**Raster to Polygon**" window below).

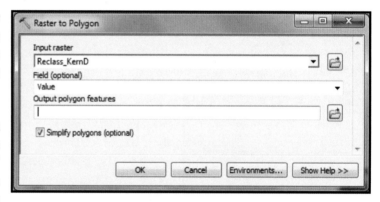

Once you have activated your "Raster to…" tool, you can begin to convert your raster map. The following steps are similar to all three tools with only minor differences specific to each.

 In the "**Input raster**" dropdown menu, select the raster map you wish to convert. From the "**Field**" dropdown menu, select the value of each cell you want saved in the Attribute table of the new shapefile. Give a name and location for the new shapefile in the "**Output polygon features**" (or polyline or point) text box.

The newly created polygon shapefile will have a unique feature for each group of contiguous cells that was in the input raster map. Each polygonal feature will also have a respective record in the shapefile's Attribute table. The attribute of each polygon will be the value of the cells that once comprised the area within it. As shown in the figure to the right, the selected polygon was once a contiguous group of cells with the value "4".

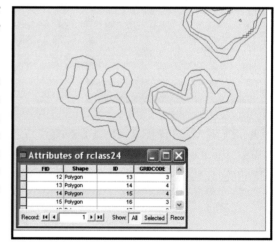

These polygonal features can be symbolized like any other vector shapefile by right-clicking on the layer in the.

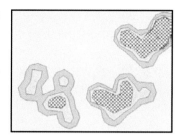

 From the Table of Contents in ArcMap: right-click the layer and select "**Properties...**" and choose the "**Symbology**" tab.

RASTER ANALYSIS/OUTPUT EXTENT

At the outset of a raster data analysis, you should define a particular study area, referred to in ArcGIS as the "processing extent". Otherwise, you might notice that some of the areas on the density raster map that you created seem to have the hotspots cut off. This occurs when the extent of the density calculation is limited to only the perimeter (i.e. extent) of the points that you are calculating the density of. Imagine this phenomenon as ArcGIS framing the output density raster map to only the smallest square box that includes all of the input points. Instead, you want the extent to be the same as the data frame

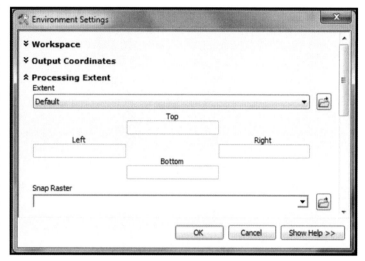

or the other shapefile layers that you are working with (such as a city outline).

 From within the window of the tool you are using (e.g. "Raster to Polygon"): click the "**Environments...**" button. Select the "**Processing Extent**" option. In the "**Extent**" dropdown, select the appropriate extent to meet your needs. If you want to use the same extent as another shapefile, add that shapefile layer to the Table of Contents in ArcMap first. The dropdown menu will provide an option for "**Same as layer...**".

CLIPPING RASTER MAPS

To clip density maps exactly to the outline of features from another shapefile, such as a city outline, you need to use a raster clipping tool. See the "**Clip**" tool discussion in Chapter 9.

 Raster Dataset file names cannot be more than 13 characters.

"NODATA" RASTER CELL VALUES

Every raster cell has a value assigned to it. Values can be either positive or negative, integer, or floating point. Cells can also have a "NoData" value to represent the absence of data. NoData means that not enough information is known about a cell location to assign it a value; or, that the cells are in areas that a user intentionally does not want to display (or wants to exclude from raster calculations). NoData and 0 are not the same; 0 is a valid value. If NoData exists in any of the input raster datasets the computation of output values can be affected in one of three ways: NoData is returned for the cell location no matter what, NoData is ignored and a value is computed using any available values, or a value is estimated for the cell location and NoData cannot be returned.

 By default, NoData values are displayed transparent in a raster map. **To change the symbology, from ArcMap:** right-click on the raster layer, click "**Properties**…", select the "**Symbology**" tab. Click the "**Display NoData as**" drop-down arrow and select a color.

RASTER CALCULATOR

The "Raster Calculator" operation in the Spatial Analyst tool creates a new grid on which the value of each cell is computed by applying map algebra and/or logical functions to the value of the cell on one or more existing grids. Essentially, it produces a new composite map. Map algebra is a general set of conventions, capabilities, and techniques that have been widely adopted for use with a GIS. Consider, for example, the three raster (grid) layers shown below. In each layer, cell values range from 0 to 3. If Raster Calculator were to be used to add each cell's values on these three grids, the result would be a composite raster map with cell values (potentially) ranging from 0 to 9.

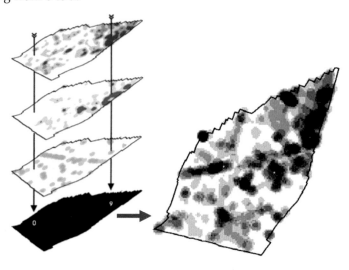

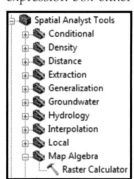 **From ArcToolbox:** click "**Spatial Analyst Tools**", select "**Map Algebra**" and activate "**Raster Calculator**". Variables (in the form of grid layers and/or numbers) and functions are inserted into the expression box either by typing, by double-clicking on the layer names in the "Layers" section, or by using the buttons. Once an expression has been fully specified, click the "Evaluate" button to generate a new grid.

The "Raster Calculator" dialog box provides for building algebra-like expressions that will produce new maps. Logical expressions prove to be either true or false for any given cell. These results are stored in the form of a new grid on which every cell is either set to 1 (for true) or 0 (for false).

NEIGHBORHOOD STATISTICS[17]

Neighborhood statistics creates a new grid in which each cell's value is computed by applying a specified statistical function to the values of an existing grid that are associated with a neighborhood of surrounding cells. This neighborhood may be in any of a variety of shapes and/or sizes. Unlike previous versions of ArcGIS, neighborhood statistics are divided into different tools in ArcGIS 10. Due to the similarities between most of the neighborhood tools, we will only show and discuss the "**Block Statistics**" tool.

From ArcToolbox: click the "**Spatial Analyst Tools**", select "**Neighborhood**" and choose the appropriate tool. **Or, From the "Block Statistics" dialog box**: specify your "**Input raster**" data. In the "**Output raster**" text box, write down the name of the new raster map. In the "**Neighborhood**" dropdown menu, specify the shape of the neighborhoods. Then in the "**Neighborhood Settings**" section, specify the size (the number of cells or map units) of the neighborhoods. In the "**Statistic type**" dropdown menu, select the statistic with which the input values are to be summarized.

Neighborhood Statistics Operations

- The **sum** statistic computes a new value for each cell by adding the existing value of that cell to those of its adjacent neighbors.
- The **mean** statistic computes a new value for each cell by averaging the existing value of that cell with those of its adjacent neighbors.
- The **median** statistic selects whichever of the values in the immediate vicinity of that cell comes closest to being equal to or just greater than those of half the others.
- The **maximum** statistic computes a new value for each cell by selecting the greatest value to occur within its immediate vicinity.
- The **minimum** statistic computes a new value for each cell by selecting the lowest value to occur within its immediate vicinity.
- The **majority** statistic computes a new value for each cell by selecting whichever value occurs most frequently within its immediate vicinity. If two or more values tie for that distinction, a value of NoData is assigned.
- The **minority** statistic computes a new value for each cell by selecting whichever value occurs least frequently within its immediate vicinity. If two or more values tie for that distinction, a value of NoData (black) is assigned.
- The **range** statistic computes a new value for each cell by subtracting the lowest value from the greatest value to occur within its immediate vicinity.
- The **STD** statistic computes a new value for each cell by calculating the mean of the squared differences between the average of all values (standard deviation) in its immediate vicinity and each original value.
- The **variety** statistic computes a new value for each cell by determining how many different conditions occur within its immediate vicinity.

DISTANCE OPERATIONS[18]

Euclidean Distance measures straight-line distance (from cell center to cell center) from each cell to the closest source; the source identifies the objects of interest, such as roads or a school. The **Cost Weighted Distance** tool equates distance as a cost factor—the cost to travel through any given cell. For example, it may be shorter to (illegally) travel through a private property to get to a destination, but it is less risky (i.e., lower cost) to walk around it. **Path distance** calculates, for each cell, the least accumulative cost distance to the nearest source, while taking into account surface distance and horizontal and vertical cost factors. **Corridor** calculates the sum of accumulative costs for two accumulative cost raster inputs.

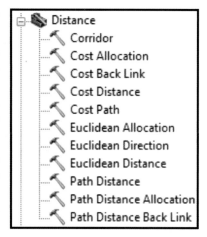

All the distance operations are within the "**Distance**" toolset.

 From ArcToolbox: click "**Spatial Analyst Tools**", select "**Distance**" and then choose the appropriate tool.

Euclidean Distance

The "**Euclidean Distance**" creates a new grid in which each cell's value indicates its "straight-line" distance between the center of that cell and the center of the nearest of a designated set of cells on an existing grid. The units of distance are map units associated with the coordinate system of the source layer.

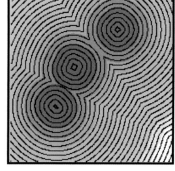

 From "**Spatial Analyst Tools**", select "**Distance**" and choose "**Euclidean Distance**". Select the "**Input raster or feature source data**", create an "**Output distance raster**" name and location and set the "**Maximum distance**" for each cell. Lastly, set the "**Output cell size**" and "**Output direction raster**", if necessary.

Euclidean Allocation

The allocation option creates a new grid in which each cell is set to the value of the nearest of a designated set of source cells on an existing grid (or source features of points, lines, or polygons) based on Euclidean distance. Here, every cell has been set to the value of the nearest Drug-Free School Zone. This "zoning" of the landscape that is generated by this operation are variously referred to as "proximal zones", "Voronoi regions", Wigner-Seitz cells", "post office areas", and "Thiessen Polygons".

 From "**Spatial Analyst Tools**", select "**Distance**" and choose "**Euclidean Allocation**". Select the "**Input raster or feature source data**", select the "**Source field**", create an "**Output distance raster**"

name and location and set the "**Maximum distance**" for each cell. Lastly, set the "**Output cell size**", "**Output distance raster**" and "**Output direction raster**", if necessary.

Cost Distance/Cost Allocation

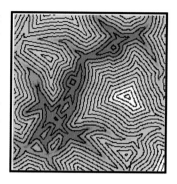

The cost distance operation is similar to the "straight line" option in that nearness is defined in terms of distances that are measured horizontally from the center of each cell to the center of the nearest source cell. However, with the Cost Distance option, those distances are not measured in units such as feet or meters. Instead, they are measured in units such as minutes, gallons of fuel, or risk of apprehension. These are not merely units of physical separation but units of <u>cost</u> that accumulate as a consequence of motion across a physical environment. Cost allocation calculates for each individual cell its nearest source based on the least accumulative cost over a cost surface.

Since the windows for cost distance and cost allocation are similar, one description is provided here.

From "**Spatial Analyst Tools**", select "**Distance**", and choose "**Cost Distance**" (or "**Cost Allocation**"). Select the "**Input raster or feature source data**", create an "**Output distance raster**" name and location and set the "**Input cost raster**". You define the "cost" to move through each cell in the "Input cost raster". You can also set the "**Maximum distance**" for each cell and the "**Output backlink raster**".

Path Distance/Path Allocation

The path distance operation generates a shapefile of one or more lines that trace the path(s) of minimum cost between designated "source" and "destination" areas. The operation is closely related to the cost distance operation and, in fact, relies on that operation to calculate the costs to be minimized. The destination layer can either be a shapefile of point, line, or polygon features (in which case the destination feature(s) should be selected), or a raster grid (in which case a destination zone should either be selected or just set to any value other than NoData). Path allocation calculates the nearest source for each cell based on the least accumulative cost over a cost surface, while taking into account surface distance and horizontal and vertical cost factors.

Since the windows for path distance/path allocation are similar, one description is provided here.

From "**Spatial Analyst Tools**", select "**Distance**", and choose "**Cost Distance**" (or "**Cost Allocation**"). Select the "**Input raster or feature source data**", create an "**Output distance raster**" name and location and set the "**Input cost raster**". You define the "cost" to move through each cell in the "Input cost raster". Define the "**Horizontal factor parameters**" and "**Vertical factor parameters**", if necessary.

ARCSCENE 3D MODELING

What most distinguishes ArcScene from the other ArcGIS applications is its ability to place layers in a three-dimensional setting. ArcScene may be used to explore the relationship of two variables in one map by adding a third-dimension. The third dimension allows you to explore the relationship between two separate attributes of a single polygon shapefile, for instance. Although this 3D map can be exported as a 2D image, this technique is recommended here more for exploration of GIS data layers and variables, not as a final map.

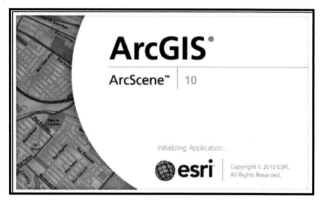

Adding Shapefile Layers

 From the Standard toolbar: click "**File**" and select "**Add Data**". **Or, From the Tools toolbar**: click ✛

You can also click and drag shapefiles right into ArcScene: From ArcMap: click on the layer in the Table of Contents and hold down and drag to the Table of Contents in ArcScene and let go.

Removing Layers from ArcScene

 From the Table of Contents: right-click the layer you wish to remove and select "**Remove**".

Layer Properties

 From the Table of Contents: right-click the layer you wish to work with and select "**Properties…**"

The "**Layer Properties**" dialog box offers more options—compared to the number offered in ArcCatalog or ArcMap. Most tabs/options should already be familiar to you from working in ArcMap (if not, see earlier chapters of this document).

Under the "**Extrusion**" tab you can turn point features into vertical lines, lines into walls, and polygons into blocks.

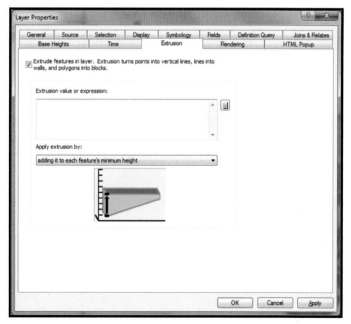

Under the "**Base Heights**" tab, you can set the height of continuous surfaces based on a constant value or by referencing one or more attributes so the height can vary from feature to feature. For example, the figure to the right is a raster map whose cells are elevated based on the density of social services throughout the city. Darker shades of blue represent areas with higher concentrations of people living at or below poverty. This map is one way to communicate that the poverty population in the city does not tend to live near where the highest concentrations of social services are located.

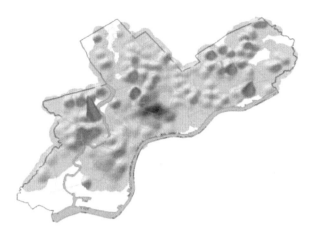

 The "Navigate" tool on the "Tools" toolbar lets you rotate the display about two axes: one running left to right through the cartographic plane, and the other running perpendicular to it.

 Refer to ArcGIS Desktop Help for more information about using ArcScene.

CHAPTER ELEVEN

Identifying Significant Patterns and Hot Spots

NEAREST NEIGHBOR ANALYSIS

The Average Nearest Neighbor tool in ArcGIS is used to perform a Nearest Neighbor (NN) analysis. The NN analysis is a test of spatial randomness and works by calculating the distance from each point in a collection to its nearest neighboring point. For polygon or line features, the NN analysis measures the distance between each feature's centroid and its nearest neighbor's centroid location. These distances are then compared to the expected mean NN distance for a random distribution of points. If the average distance is less than the average for a hypothetical random distribution, then the features being analyzed are considered clustered. If the average distance is greater than a hypothetical random distribution, the features are considered dispersed. The equation in ArcGIS used to calculate the average NN value, Z score, and p-value are based on the assumption that the points being measured are free to locate anywhere within the study area (i.e. all points are located independently of one another).

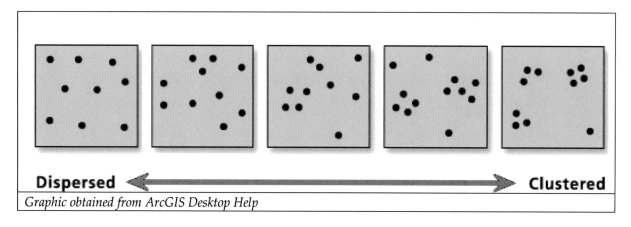

Dispersed ⟵   ⟶ **Clustered**

Graphic obtained from ArcGIS Desktop Help

The Average Nearest Neighbor tool was used to determine whether the high-risk (polygon/vector) cells in the Period 1 Risk Terrain (right) were statistically significantly clustered. Results suggest that there is less than one percent likelihood that the clustered pattern of high risk cells could be the result of random chance (Observed/Expected Mean Distance = 0.63; Z Score = -14.33 standard deviations; Critical Value = -2.58; $p<0.01$). Although this is quite evident upon visual inspection, the pattern is *statistically significant*. Other patterns may not be so obvious.

The pin map on the next page is another example. It shows incident locations of DWI arrests during 2008. If motor vehicle stops that result in DWI arrests cluster in certain areas of the city, then police patrols and interventions such as sobriety checkpoints are warranted, and can be more easily and efficiently

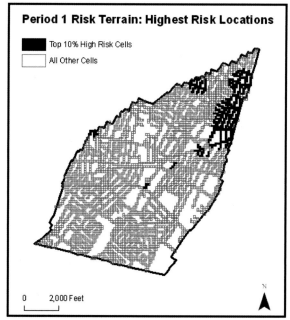

Period 1 Risk Terrain: Highest Risk Locations

■ Top 10% High Risk Cells
□ All Other Cells

0   2,000 Feet

N

targeted to the high-risk locations. Results of a NN analysis suggest that the distribution of DWI arrest locations is significantly clustered (z score= -10.31; R=0.33; $p<0.05$; Mean NN Dist.=348.07; Exp. Mean NN

Dist.=1065.90). A density map or standard deviation ellipse might be used to show how and where DWI arrests are concentrated in particular areas.

From ArcToolbox: click "**Spatial Statistics Tools**", select "**Analyzing Patterns**" and activate the "**Average Nearest Neighbor**" tool.

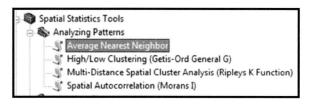

Once you have opened the "Average Nearest Neighbor" tool, you can begin your analysis:

From the "**Average Nearest Neighbor**" dialog box, select your input shapefile for which the average NN index will be calculated in the "**Input Feature Class**". This is typically a point shapefile, but can be line or polygon shapefile as well. You will need to specify how distances between features should be calculated. "**EUCLIDEAN_DISTANCE**" is the default and most commonly used. It measures straight-line distances ('as the crow flies').

DWI Arrest Locations 2008 (n=59)

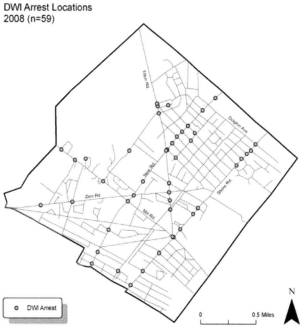

o   DWI Arrest

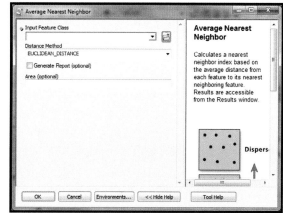

ZOOM IN: Parole Officer Caseloads[19]

Mellow, Schlager, and Caplan (2008) randomly selected parole officers' caseloads from the Newark, NJ region to investigate their distribution and overlap. Minimum convex polygons (MCP) were used to show the smallest perimeter within which each of these caseloads was distributed (see below, left). Further analysis revealed that caseloads were inefficiently distributed and had a high degree of overlap:

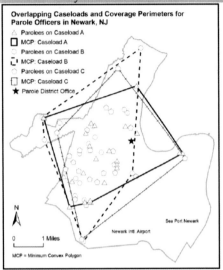

Parole officer (PO) A's case load of 24 parolees represented just 4% of the total study sample, but was distributed to a perimeter of 13.49 miles and covered an area of 11 square miles, or 45% of the total Newark study area; PO B's case load of 24 parolees represented just 4% of the total study sample, but was distributed to a perimeter of 14.85 miles and covered an area of 13 square miles, or 53% of the total study area; PO C's case load of 18 parolees represented just 3% of the total study sample, but was distributed to a perimeter of 15.41 miles and covered an area of 13 square miles, or 49% of the total study area.

Related to overlap, clustering of PO caseloads should be a logistical concern for parole agencies because the geographic distribution of parolees within a caseload is an enabling factor for parole officers to serve as efficient and effective case managers and supervisors. Therefore, it was hypothesized by Mellow et al. that the residential locations of parolees within the same caseload would be spatially clustered together in certain parts of Newark. This was not the case. Nearest Neighbor analyses validated the researchers' conclusion that regardless of caseload size, parolees within a given caseload were randomly dispersed throughout Newark without any regard to geographic clustering. A random distribution suggested no forethought on the part of the parole agency to assign caseloads based on the geographic location of parolee residences. On average, parolees on the same case load resided ten times farther apart from each other than the "natural" geographic distribution of all parolee residences within Newark.

Through a hypothetic-deductive process that utilized GIS, Mellow et al. concluded that a revised system of caseload allocation based on the natural distribution of parolee residences could save time, money and resources for parole officers and their agencies. The study also provided empirical evidence that GIS is an instrumental tool for use in the parole system.

STANDARD DEVIATION ELLIPSES

This section was adapted or excerpted directly from: ArcGIS Desktop Help files.

 From ArcToolbox: click "**Spatial Statistics Tools**", select "**Measuring Geographic Distributions**" and activate the "**Directional Distribution (Standard Deviational Ellipse)**" tool.

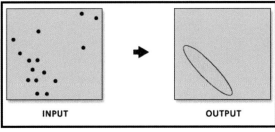

A Standard Deviational Ellipse (SDE) can be used to measure central tendency of a set of points, lines or polygons. A SDE identifies dispersion as the standard deviation of the distance of each feature location from the mean center, as well as the direction of that dispersion. The mean center, or central location, refers to the arithmetic mean of all feature locations (centroids are used in the case of line or polygon features). The ellipse is referred to as the standard deviation ellipse because the method calculates the standard deviation of the x coordinates and y coordinates of each feature from the mean center to define the outer bounds of a smoothed ellipse polygon, which is displayed as a map feature. The attribute values for a SDE include two standard distances (long and short axes), the orientation of the ellipse, and the case field, if specified. The "Directional Distribution" tool in ArcGIS creates SDEs.

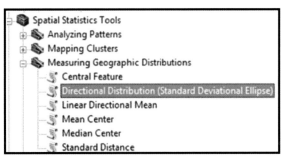

 In the "Directional Distribution" window, select a shapefile to be the "**Input Feature Class**". This should contain the set of points, lines, or polygons for which the SDE will be calculated. In the "**Output Ellipse Feature Class**" field, choose a name and location for the new polygon shapefile that will contain the output ellipse feature. Choose the size of the output ellipse in the "**Ellipse Size**" drop down menu. The default is 1 standard deviation (SD); available options are 1, 2, or 3. With features normally distributed around the mean center, one SD will cover approximately 68 percent of all input feature centroids. Two SDs will cover approximately 95 percent of all feature centroids. Three SDs will cover approximately 99 percent of all feature centroids. The optional "**Weight Field**" permits the weighting of locations according to their relative importance; it is based on a value in the input shapefile's attribute table. The resulting ellipse is termed a weighted SDE. The optional

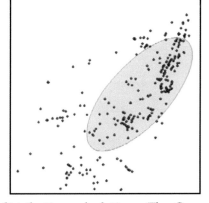

"**Case Field**" can be used to group features for separate directional distribution calculations. The Case Field can be of numeric, date, or string type.

HOT SPOT ANALYSIS (Getis-Ord Gi*)

From ArcToolbox: click "**Spatial Statistics Tools**", select "**Mapping Clusters**" and activate "**Hot Spot Analysis (Getis-Ord Gi*)**".

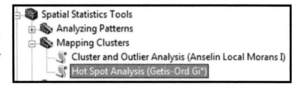

Your choice of symbology and classification schemes might imply areas that some people would call "hotspots" upon visual inspection alone. However, this terminology should be used cautiously. The (often) arbitrary choice of colors and classification ranges, or the classification method (e.g. Equal Interval, Natural Breaks, Standard Deviation) could substantially change a map's appearance. For this reason, a "hotspot" defined upon visual inspection is much different than a "statistically significant hotspot". To be statistically significant, a feature must have a high value and be surrounded by other features with high values. Similarly, cold spots consist of features with low values surrounded by other features with low values. This pattern must occur beyond random chance.

The "Hot Spot Analysis" tool in ArcGIS calculates the Getis-Ord Gi* statistic (Z score) for each feature in a dataset. The larger the statistically significant positive Z score is, the more intense the clustering of high values (hotspot). The smaller the statistically significant negative Z score is, the more intense the clustering of low values (coldspot).

The default selections in the "Hot Spot Analysis" dialog box are recommended. The "**Input Feature Class**" (shapefile) must have an analysis field (Input Field). The tool assesses whether high or low values (e.g. the number of crimes per polygon; number of victims for each point) cluster spatially. The "**Input Field**" containing those values is your analysis field. Prepare this field in the shapefile's attribute table before using the "Hot Spot Analysis" tool. Within the "**Conceptualization of Spatial Relationships**" dropdown menu, select the spatial relationship among

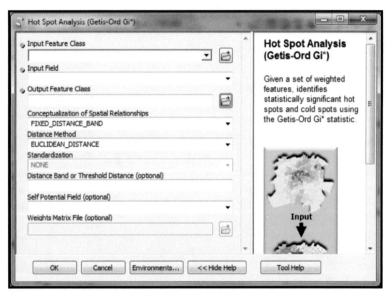

features. Output from this tool may look similar to the example map below—where red colored cells represent statistically significant hot spots of "high risk" locations, and blue colored cells represent statistically significant cold spots of "low risk" locations.

How you construct the analysis field determines the types of questions that can be asked. For example, if you divide the number of burglaries by the number of houses in a city, and then run the Hot Spot Analysis tool on this ratio, you are no longer asking "Where are there a lot of burglaries?" Instead, you are asking "Where are there unexpectedly high numbers of burglaries, given the number of houses?" By creating a rate or ratio prior to analysis, you can control for certain relationships and possibly identify unexpected hot or cold spots.

⚠ *ArcGIS Desktop Help presents "3 things to consider when undertaking any hot spot analysis". You should review this help section by searching for keywords "How hot spot analysis works" > click to view the first topic found.*

SPATIAL AUTOCORRELATION BASICS

Distributions among geographical units are usually not independent, meaning that values found in a particular location are likely to be influenced by corresponding values in nearby locations. Imagine, for instance, that a home's value will be more affected by the value of neighboring houses compared to houses that are farther away: Houses that are on one side of town tend to have less effect on the value of a house far away on the opposite side of town. Stated another way: things tend to be influenced by other things that are closer to them, compared to other things that are farther away. This phenomenon is referred to as spatial autocorrelation.

When testing the predictive validity of spatial data, you may have to control for spatial autocorrelation. Again, this refers to feature similarity based on both feature locations and feature values simultaneously. Or stated another way, spatial autocorrelation refers to the degree to which cells within spatial features (e.g. census tracts) and their associated values (e.g., the dependent variable: crime counts) tend to be clustered together throughout the landscape (i.e. positive spatial autocorrelation) or dispersed (i.e. negative spatial autocorrelation). Note that spatial autocorrelation--for the purposes of testing predictive validity--is measured using the dependent variable (i.e. the outcome events) and not the independent variable. Controlling for spatial autocorrelation allows you to measure the effect of a place on the attraction of outcome events without the similar patterns of outcome events in neighboring places confounding your results.

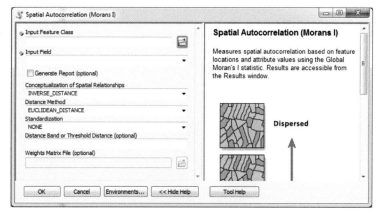

Moran's I is an area-wide analysis used to measure spatial autocorrelation. ArcGIS has a "**Spatial Autocorrelation (Moran's I)**" tool in ArcToolbox that can be used to measure spatial autocorrelation, with values approaching 1 when geographical units are situated near other similar geographical units, and approaching –1 when geographical units are situated near dissimilar geographical units. A Moran's I value of 0 indicates the absence of autocorrelation, or independence, among geographical units. If spatial autocorrelation exists, then you should create a spatial lag control variable to include in your statistical model.

NOTES ON STATISTICAL TESTING WHEN PLACES ARE THE UNITS OF ANALYSIS

There are several reasonable ways to empirically test the validity of a spatial data, including OLS, logistic, or geographically weighted (GW) regression models. Some of these methods are shown in the table below. ArcGIS currently provides tools for OLS and Geographically Weighted Regression modeling. An informative resource for these tools is available here: http://resources.arcgis.com/gallery/file/geoprocessing /details?entryID=8901F5BD-1422-2418-88FE-592BA3458CAF

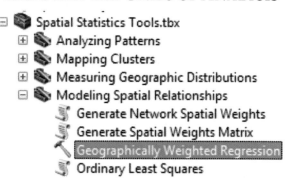

The most appropriate method for statistical testing will depend on a variety of things, including the nature of your outcome events data, type/size of units of analysis, and the way you prepare your data (i.e. binary or interval values). You are encouraged to explore different empirical methods that suit your needs the best.

CHAPTER TWELVE

Online Mapping and ArcGIS.com

ONLINE MAPPING

Online mapping has generated a lot of attention in the last couple of years. This can be attributed to several factors, including the ease and accessibility of online mapping software and the increased use of servers to store and collect data. Online mapping is a beneficial asset for most organizations as it allows its users to share information with other users in an efficient manner. In some cases, it also allows users to manipulate online data for their own purposes.

WHAT IS ARCGIS.COM?

The ability for users to take advantage of online mapping has been incorporated in the newest version of ArcGIS. **ArcGIS.com** is a new website that allows users to create an online (web) map using one or more different map services. Not only does it allow users to create maps, but it also provides an avenue for users to share their maps to other users as well as be a place for users to store their maps. Importantly, no ArcGIS software needs to actually be installed on a user's computer in order for an online map to be made; however, any map made on ArcGIS.com can be incorporated within ArcMap 10. ArcGIS.com is free to register and use.

Accessing ArcGIS.com

 From your web browser: type www.arcgis.com in the address bar. **Or, From the Standard toolbar in ArcMap**: click "**File**" and select "**ArcGIS Online…**".

You'll notice that opening ArcGIS.com through a web browser and through ArcMap leads to a different interface:

Interface when opened through ArcMap 10   Interface when opened through web browser

Despite looking different, both interfaces have the same basic actions. Both provide a search bar, which allows you to search ArcGIS online, and an area for you to sign-in. In general, you can consider the ArcMap's version of the ArcGIS online interface as being a condensed form of the web interface.

Registering/Sign-in for ArcGIS.com

Technically, you can use ArcGIS.com without registering; however, your activities are limited. It may be more beneficial for you to register for ArcGIS.com (it's free!). By registering, you can save (you are allotted up to 2 GB of storage space) and share your interactive maps and create and join groups.

 From your web browser: type in www.ArcGIS.com in the address bar. Click on the "**Sign in**" option in the upper right. **Or, From ArcMap**: click "**File**" on the Standard toolbar and select "**ArcGIS Online…**". Click "**Sign in**". The "**ArcGIS Online Sign in**" window will appear. Sign--in or if you are opening a new account, click "**Get new account**". This will take you to the ArcGIS.com website.

WORKING WITH MAPS IN ARCGIS.COM

ArcGIS Map Viewer interface

Think of the ArcGIS Map Viewer interface as a very basic version of ArcMap. You can create, view and save maps that are made using a base map and other additional layers found in ArcGIS.com – all for free.

ArcGIS Explorer Online Interface

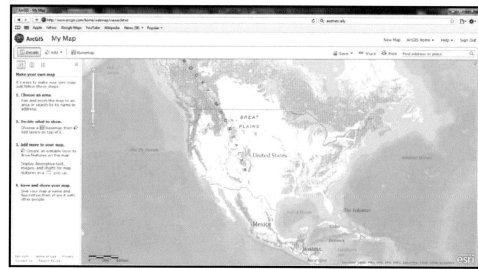

The ArcGIS Explorer Online is a step-up from the Map Viewer. It provides you with more functions and tools. Additionally, it also allows you to create a presentation (similar to a power point presentation) of your maps. You can access this free interface at http://explorer.arcgis.com/

 In order to run the Explorer online interface, you need Silverlight plug-in from Microsoft.

ArcGIS Explorer Desktop

Explorer desktop is a further step up in functionality. Unlike the Map Viewer and Explorer online, Explorer Desktop runs more like a software program (like ArcMap) as opposed to an online server. In addition to the tools and functions of Map Viewer and Explorer online, you are able to include shapefiles and other data sources. In addition, you can view maps in 3D.

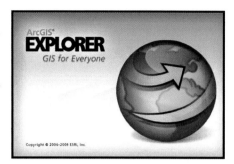

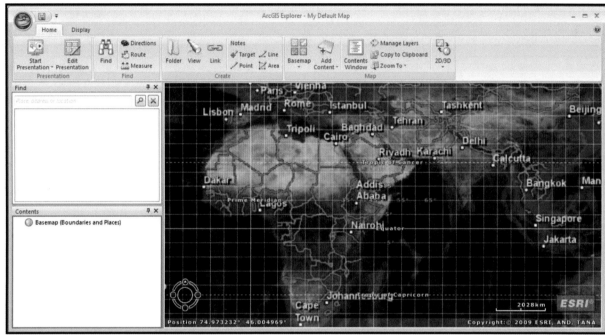

ArcGIS for iOS

If you have an iOS device (i.e. iPad), you can download ArcGIS for iOS for free. This application allows you to view your maps and conduct very simple GIS functions.

ArcGIS Desktop (ArcMap 10)

 From the Standard toolbar: click "**File**", select "**Add Data**" and choose "**Add Data From ArcGIS Online…**".

Or, From the Tools toolbar: click 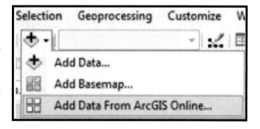 and select "**Add Data from ArcGIS Online…**".

Use ArcGIS.com data as you would any other type of data we have discussed in this book.

Working with ArcGIS.com files

Uploading Files
You can upload a map document (.mxd) or a layer package (.lpk) to ArcGIS.com.

 Sign-in to ArcGIS.com. Click the "**My Content**" tab and select the "**Add Item**" button. The "Add Item" window will appear. Choose "**a file on my computer**" within the "**The Item is**" dropdown. Choose a file within "**File**". Provide a "**Title**" and any appropriate "**Tags**".

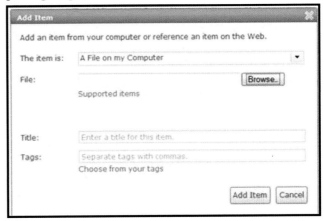

⚠ *Remember to only upload files that you are allowed to upload. In other words, do not upload any files with any confidential or protected information.*

Editing a File
 Sign-in to ArcGIS.com. Click "**My Content**" tab and click the title of the item you wish to edit. Click the "**Edit**" button (on the left).

Sharing a File
You can upload and share a file with the general public. Such information can be viewed by people who are not registered or using ArcGIS.com.

  Sign-in to ArcGIS.com. Click "**My Content**" tab and check the box beside the item you want to share. Click the "**Select**" button (see left). The "**Share**" window will appear. Click the box beside "**Everyone (public)**". If you wish to share the file with a group, and check the box next to the group(s) you want to share the file with.

⚠ *Once you have uploaded an item in ArcGIS.com, you can provide a URL to the item. This can be linked to emails, blogs, websites and social networking sites (e.g. Facebook).*

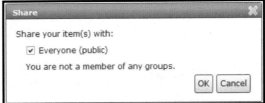

Deleting a File

 Sign-in to ArcGIS.com. Click "**My Content**" tab and click the box beside the title you wish to delete. Click "**Delete**" (on the left).

SHARING MAPS

As discussed earlier, one of the benefits of ArcGIS.com is the ability for users to share the maps they create with others.

Linking to a Map

  From the Map interface: click the "**Share**" option. The "**Share**" window will appear. You have the option of clicking the "**Share with everyone (public)**" and you also have the ability to directly post to Facebook and/or Twitter. Note, that when you click the "Share with everyone" option, the "**Embed this map**" options become active. In addition, you can also obtain the link for the map for email or IM.

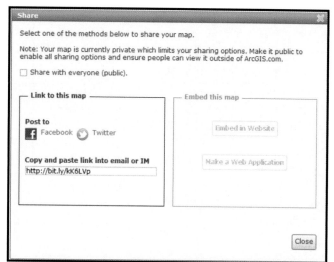

Making a Web Application

 From the "**Share**" window, click the "**Make a Web Application**" option. The "**Make a Web Application**" window will open. Select a template and click "**Download**" (or "**Preview**" if you just want to preview the template). You will be prompted to download a .zip file. Unzip the file and follow the instructions provided (as a readme.html).

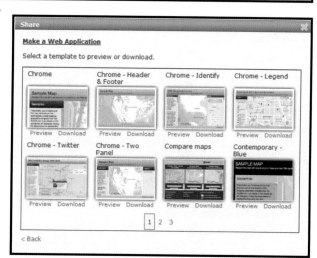

GROUPS IN ARCGIS.COM

ArcGIS.com is very much an online community as it is a mapping tool. Joining, creating and participating in groups is an easy way for you to obtain and share information. You can be part of a public or private group.

Joining a Group

 Sign-in to ArcGIS.com. Click "**Groups**". Use the search toolbar to search for a particular group or click "**List all public groups**" to bring up a list of groups you can join.

Creating a Group

 Sign-in to ArcGIS.com. Click "**Groups**" and select the "**Create a Group**" button. Provide a name for the group and a thumbnail image. Provide a summary and description for the group. Under "**Status**" determine whether you want the group "**Public**" or "**Private**". Lastly, choose appropriate tags for the group.

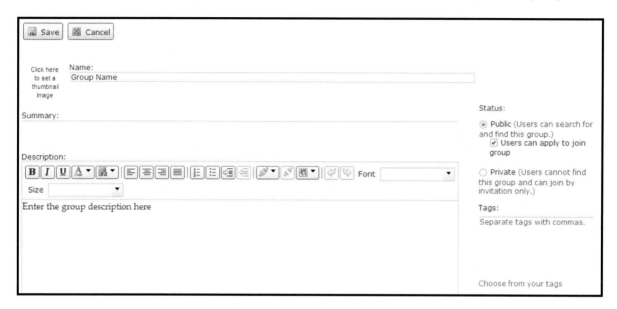

Tools and Functions

You may be wondering why we have not covered any of the tools and functions of ArcGIS.com. As many of the functions within the ArcGIS.com interfaces are similar to the tools and functions we've discussed already in this guide, we decided not to repeat them in this section. Refer to the appropriate tool in this guide that is discussed for ArcMap or ArcCatalog to use for ArcGIS.com; however, keep in mind that minor differences may exist. For more information on using ArcGIS.com, see the following link to access the ArcGIS resource center:

http://help.arcgis.com/en/arcgisonline/help/index.html#/Overview/010q00000002000000/

ADDING MAP LAYERS TO GOOGLE EARTH

This is a great way to present finished maps. It can also be useful for exploring street-level environmental contexts. See the most up-to-date tutorial for exporting KML/KMZ (Google Earth compatible) files at:

www.rutgerscps.org/docs/MapLayerToGoogle Earth_Tutorial.pdf

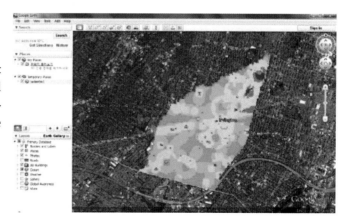

ADDITIONAL SPATIAL ANALYSIS AND STATISTICAL SOFTWARE

CrimeStat
FREE | Available at: http://www.icpsr.umich.edu/CRIMESTAT
CrimeStat is a Windows-based spatial statistics program for the analysis of crime incident locations (point patterns). The program inputs incident locations in .dbf, .shp, ASCII or ODBC-compliant formats using either spherical or projected coordinates. It can then calculate various spatial statistics and write graphical objects in shapefile format. *CrimeStat* is a popular tool for researchers, police departments and other public safety practitioners.

GeoDa
FREE | Available at: https://geodacenter.asu.edu/
GeoDa is a freestanding software application that does not require a specific GIS system. It consists of an interactive environment that combines maps with statistical graphics, using the technology of dynamically linked windows. GeoDa is often used to analyze aggregated crime data (area patterns); but it also has a spatial regression package included that allows for the modeling of correlates or determinants of crime.

For a detailed, but introductory, discussion of the functionality of CrimeStat and GeoDa, see pages 43-63 of *Eck, J. E., Chainey, S. Cameron, J. G., Leitner, M., & Wilson, R. E. (2005).* Mapping crime: Understanding hot spots. *Washington, D.C.: National Institute of Justice.* Available at:
http://www.ncjrs.gov/pdffiles1/nij/209393.pdf

SchoolCop
FREE | Available at: http://www.schoolcopsoftware.com
The School Crime Operations Package (*School COP*) is a FREE software application for entering, analyzing, and mapping incidents that occur in and around schools. *School COP* can include incident data from a single school or several schools (for example, schools in a district). Target users include school security staff, school police departments, school resource officers, and school administrative staff. *School COP* can produce maps showing the location of incidents within school buildings or on school grounds and it can produce an assortment of graphs, including bar graphs and pie charts. It also includes a variety of pre-formatted tabular reports, including reports that summarize a specific incident or set of incidents and that aggregate incidents by month or school.

SPACE (Spatial Predictive Analysis of Crime Extension)
FREE | Available at: http://www.bairsoftware.com/space/
SPACE is an extension for Esri's ArcGIS application that provides tools optimized for crime analysis and for analyzing and predicting spatial information.

Epi Info

FREE | Available at: http://wwwn.cdc.gov/epiinfo/

Created by the Centers for Disease Control and Prevention (CDC), EpiInfo is a free-standing statistical software application. In short, the software does a lot of advanced statistical analyses that may be useful to analyze and interpret your mapping results. EpiInfo also has some GIS capabilities as well.

ENDNOTES

---

[1] Adapted from: http://law.justia.com/us/cfr/title41/41-3.1.1.2.13.8.175.6.8.html

[2] Stoe, D. A. (2003). Using Geographic Information Systems To Map Crime Victim Services: A Guide for State Victims of Crime Act Administrators and Victim Service Providers. U.S. Department of Justice: Washington, DC.

[3] Adapted from: Chainey, S. & Ratcliffe, J. (2005). *GIS and Crime Mapping*. Wiley: West Sussex, England

[4] Adapted from: Chainey, S. & Ratcliffe, J. (2005). *GIS and Crime Mapping*. Wiley: West Sussex, England

[5] Adapted from: Chainey, S. & Ratcliffe, J. (2005). *GIS and Crime Mapping*. Wiley: West Sussex, England

[6] Adapted from: Chainey, S. & Ratcliffe, J. (2005). *GIS and Crime Mapping*. Wiley: West Sussex, England

[7] Chainey, S. & Ratcliffe, J. (2005). *GIS and Crime Mapping*. Wiley: West Sussex, England

[8] Adapted from: Chainey, S. & Ratcliffe, J. (2005). *GIS and Crime Mapping*. Wiley: West Sussex, England

[9] Adapted from: Chainey, S. & Ratcliffe, J. (2005). *GIS and Crime Mapping*. Wiley: West Sussex, England

[10] Adapted from: Chainey, S. & Ratcliffe, J. (2005). *GIS and Crime Mapping*. Wiley: West Sussex, England

[11] From: http://webhelp.esri.com/arcgisdesktop/9.2/index.cfm?id=1430&pid=1427&topicname=How_and_when_to_use_attribute_tables

[12] Adapted from: Ormsby, E., Napoleon, E., Burke, R., Groess, C., & Feaster, L. (2001). Getting to know ArcGIS Desktop (2nd ed.). Redlands, CA: ESRI.

[13] This section was adapted from content provided by: Ahmet Rahmi Kirkpinar, Graduate Student (2009), Rutgers University, School of Criminal Justice.

[14] This section was inspired by work produced by Jerry Ratcliffe and some of its content was adapted or excerpted from http://www.jratcliffe.net/

[15] Ratcliffe, J. H. (2004). Geocoding crime and a first estimate of a minimum acceptable hit rate. International Journal of Geographical Information Science, 18, 61-72.

[16] Metraux, S., Caplan, J. M., Klugman, D., & Hadley, T. R. (2007). Assessing Residential Segregation Among Medicaid Recipients with Psychiatric Disability in Philadelphia. *Journal of Community Psychology, 35*(2), p. 239-255.

[17] Some of the content of this section was adapted or excerpted from work produced by Dana Tomlin.

[18] Some of the content of this section was adapted or excerpted from work produced by Dana Tomlin.

[19] Mellow, J., Schlager, M. D., & Caplan, J. M. (2008). Using GIS to evaluate post-release prisoner services in Newark, New Jersey. *Journal of Criminal Justice, 36*(5).